To Leo

with high regard of

Omar abu Knanth.

—

BUSINESS PRACTICES, TRADE POSITION, AND COMPETITION

BUSINESS PRACTICES,
TRADE POSITION,
AND COMPETITION

By OSWALD KNAUTH

19 56

COLUMBIA UNIVERSITY PRESS

NEW YORK

© 1956 COLUMBIA UNIVERSITY PRESS, NEW YORK

*Published in Great Britain, Canada, India, and Pakistan
by Geoffrey Cumberlege: Oxford University Press,
London, Toronto, Bombay, and Karachi*

Library of Congress Catalog Card Number: 56-8555

MANUFACTURED IN THE UNITED STATES OF AMERICA

ACKNOWLEDGMENTS

MY GRATITUDE is due many people who have kindly given of their time and advice. George Soule advised in the original layout of the chapters and brought order out of confusion. William Bridgwater contributed of his skill in clarifying some obscure passages. Miss Lynette Jones and Miss Vergene Leverenz edited the entire manuscript. Those who contributed of their knowledge in their special fields are: Wroe Alderson, C. Canby Balderston, Solomon Barkin, Murray Benedict, Percival R. Brundage, Randolph Burgess, Arthur F. Burns, William H. Davis, Joel Dean, Thurlow M. Gordon, Dexter Keezer, Arnold W. Knauth, Robert Lynd, George O. May, Barbara S. Morgan, Shepard Morgan, Boris Shishkin, John Traphagen, Gordon Wasson, and Leo Wolman. To all of them my thanks. I hasten to say they are in no way responsible for the interpretation, and I suspect that individually they would disagree with parts of it.

OSWALD KNAUTH

March, 1956

CONTENTS

BUSINESS PRACTICES, TRADE POSITION, AND COMPETITION

1

THE GREAT CHANGE
IN BUSINESS PRACTICES

AMERICAN BUSINESS PRACTICE in its present state is the result of many decisions made by many men in solving the problems immediately confronting them, created by ever changing conditions. There is no master plan behind these decisions. All are made by individuals, in the light of their experience of the past and their judgment of the future.

This system has grown spontaneously, without the theoretical background expounded by the classical economists. It is an economy of balance and innovation, managed through the foresight of administrators in industry, in finance, in labor, and in government, each adjusting as best he can to his particular circumstances. This is no perfect or self-adjusting economy. The roles that are played by the different sections of the whole may be at times contradictory, even antagonistic, yet in the end constructive.

The classical theory of economy as developed by Adam Smith and David Ricardo, followed by a long line of economists through Alfred Marshall and Frank W. Taussig, was built on a series of assumptions:

1. That there are many independent units in every industry, each without power to affect the total.

2. That each unit strives for the greatest profit in every separate transaction as its final goal.

3. That each unit is in active competition both in buying and selling.

4. That in this activity a natural price results from demand and supply.

5. That each unit in seeking its own interest furthers the general social interest.

6. That there is nearly complete mobility of capital and labor, and also free entry into or exit from any industry.

7. That scarcity of goods (taken as a whole) is normal and hence an increase in production is the goal of industry.

On these assumptions, economists erected a theoretical logical structure which indicated that a free market would allocate resources to fill the needs of consumers in the order of their preference. An equilibrium or a natural price would exist about which actual market prices would fluctuate closely. At the natural price, demand at any given time would approximately equal supply for each article. Furthermore, any change in demand or supply would be reflected in a new price which would mark a new equilibrium.

The theory of consumption showed how the demand for each kind of article would be registered in the market in the order of consumer preferences. The theory demonstrated how the desire of businessmen to make the maximum profit on each article would lead to supplying at the lowest possible price the quantity demanded of that article. As a consequence, economic resources would be harnessed to the needs of consumers. Scarce resources would be rationed through high prices.

The classical theory further showed how an economy based on these assumptions would stimulate growth. The more successful businessmen would be those more alert in satisfying wants of consumers. They would seek to reduce prices through cutting their costs; therefore they would search out the best sources of supply, install more efficient methods of production, exercise better management. This would lead to economic progress registered in a rise of real incomes.

The classical theory assumed that the economy under a free market competition would naturally approximate an equilibrium. Therefore, a lack of equilibrium at any time must be due to interference from the outside, such as a drought or other calamity, political maneuvering, or a combination creating a monopoly. The remedy was to restore and preserve free-market competition.

Even in its highest development the free enterprise system probably did not in any way approach the perfection of the theoretical analysis. Indeed Adam Smith's work was in large part inspired by a moralistic desire to point the true way in an imperfect world. In this approach he and his followers were successful, for the general judgment has long been that any deviation from this ideal concept of free competition is immoral; and, in truth, the theory was based on a solid set of facts which under then existing conditions had much to commend it. Legal theory has adopted it almost without change; but if the assumptions on which the classical theory rests are not true, the major tests which the economy must meet cannot be judged by the classical mechanisms.

Businessmen engaged in the management of large enterprises have long since rejected the classical theory as an explanation of their actions and methods. Many, though not all, economists have become increasingly restive when seeking to theorize about the free-market competitive economy. Some have looked back to that golden age with nostalgic eyes. Some economists, especially those connected with business, have rejected it completely. Others have attempted to reconcile it with the facts by adding prefixes and suggesting new standards.

With the advent of continuous mass production came the necessity for creating organized distribution. Sales became more important than production, for production depended on sales. A large and increasing part of the economy began to operate under new adaptations, and by the middle of the twentieth century approximately two thirds of the economy had split away from the free enterprise system and was functioning under rules and methods of its own making.

This segment of the economy is operated by public corporations (following the nomenclature adopted in England), whose shares are largely owned by persons not connected with the management, as distinguished from the private corporation, partnership, and individual business.

In this inquiry the word "corporation" will be used only with publicly owned corporations in mind. In this sense, "publicly owned" does not mean owned by government, but owned by a large number of private shareholders not as such connected with management.

A source of confusion lies in the grouping together of public and private corporations. These are essentially different. The public corporation has certain privileges, and its public responsibilities are more and more clearly defined and regulated. Roughly, it is identical with those whose shares are listed and traded on organized stock exchanges. There are about 3,000 of them.

The private corporation is created by the same law and has the same privileges, but it lacks public or social importance. It is economically more closely related to a trust or partnership. The relationships are limited to the participants, who act as individuals and whose influence is limited to their own resources and personalities. They are not entitled to structural permanence and privilege, for they have no widespread functional and collective responsibility. Their term of existence should be limited.

The postulates of this large and growing segment of publicly owned corporations may be described as follows:

1. It is not uncommon in any industry for a few paramount corporations to control the major part of the production. One or another sets the price; others follow.

2. The basic struggle of each unit is to survive. To survive requires the winning of a trade position which insures continuity. Profit is necessary for continuity, but not profit on each transaction. No calculation of the flow of profit can be more than a rough approximation.

3. Each company seeks unique advantages which remove it from proximate dependence on the market place. Distribution is the keynote of the economy. The rate of production depends on the rate of distribution. Prime interest centers in maintaining a level, continuous flow of production and distribution.

4. In a concern making multiple products, costs are reckoned through arbitrary assumptions. It is impossible to arrive at any exact, indisputable cost.

5. Price is calculated and announced in advance after a study of consumer desires in regard to quantity, quality, size of package, custom, cost, and like considerations.

6. The bulk of capital is fixed, "sunk" in single-purpose devices, expensive and difficult, if not impossible, to move or change.

7. Shifts in each industry occur more frequently through infiltration from a neighbor industry than from a newcomer. Freedom of entry has inherent difficulties in contrast to the many advantages of the established, going concern.

8. Not scarcity but capacity to overproduce to the point of surplus determines values, prices, processes, and judgments.

The problems, policies, and methods of today's industrialists and businessmen have been determined by efforts to meet today's necessities. They do not correspond to present legal theory, which is based on the classic economic ideology of a century ago. This antithesis between practice and law has posed serious questions, led to confused thought, and produced stopgap, generally inadequate solutions.

The manufacturing economy of the mid-nineteenth century was essentially static; that of the mid-twentieth century is dynamic; the former could stop and start, the latter is a continuous flow; the former was based on scarcity, the latter on abundance. In the former, other things remained the same, *"ceteris paribus"* had significance; in the latter, change is likely to have far-reaching, unpredictable effects.

The first attempt to analyze a changed situation is necessarily to adopt prefixes and modifications of accepted concepts. Thus complete opposition between competition and monopoly is modified. In classical theory there was either perfect competition or monopoly: one was good, the other bad; one was white, the other black. Today economists recognize shades of gray. Thus, under changed conditions, competition becomes imperfect, semimonopolistic, workable, "more or less." Monopoly becomes duopoly or oligopoly, or even a "tendency toward." Restraint of trade becomes either "reasonable" or collusive. Prices are differentiated as administered, discriminatory, follow-the-leader; they are arrived at through policies, custom, strategy, or ethics; not through face-to-face bargaining.

The former exactness of terminology has become relative and vague. Concepts shade into each other by imperceptible degrees. The inherent complexity of the economy is increased by a confusion of words and meanings. The addition of prefixes and modifications is the stage at which the courts and administrative commissions have arrived.

Accountants, in spite of their difficulties in portraying the exact position of a company in an industry, have gone one step further. The income statement has taken precedence over the balance sheet. The balance sheet represented a pinpoint of time: a static concept. The income statement reflects a flow over a period of time; it is dynamic. As a guide for action or judgment, this change which has taken place over the last twenty-five years is momentous.

The economists have advanced even farther. Aided by the great growth of statistics in recent years, they have delved deeply into the nature of the productive and distributive process. They have studied the flow of goods and money. They have measured the input and output of many industries. They have recognized the dynamic nature of the economy and have set up devices for measuring it.

The business administrators, who have been forced by the necessity of survival to adjust their acts and policies to the situations in which they found themselves, have gone the greatest distance. As they were driven to lower costs, they set up machinery for mass production. As their natural market (sometimes called the "core" demand as

distinguished from the "fringe" demand) became sur-
feited, they set about expanding it further by new inducements and by searching for new uses of their product. As
an even flow of distribution became necessary, they set
prices and qualities and developed a selling organization
on whatever terms seemed expedient. They made contracts
and arrangements to fit their practical needs. They permitted themselves the joy of self-satisfaction through their
bringing of new goods and services to a hungry population. They also took pride in creating employment for an
expanding number of workers. Naturally they gasp at being informed that they are illegal, immoral, antisocial,
monopolistic.

Administrators of large businesses know from their own
experience that they have no monopoly. While outside observers deplore the decline of competition, insiders know
that competititon is keen—perhaps keener than ever before, even becoming destructive. But when administrators
attempt to argue that they operate under the tenets of
free enterprise they are so obviously beside the mark that
a confused public accuses them of cynicism and even de-
ceit. The system that has evolved is one of enterprise, de-
manding constant innovation and realignment. But, in the
original sense, it is not "free." Rather it is "administered"
or "managed" on a long-term basis. Moreover, as will be
shown later, it is competitive and nonmonopolistic. But
these words have acquired a meaning beyond and removed
from their classical or legal sense.

The economy which has evolved is not neatly self-adjusting or logical as are the thought systems of free classical
enterprise or socialism. On the contrary, it is a system
which has grown spontaneously through the practical need

of thousands of businessmen to meet concrete problems. For purposes of evaluation there has been erected a system of business accounting, the aims of which give precision to the concepts that are useful in forming judgments. As the techniques of different businesses vary, so do the methods by which they are efficiently operated. This economy is in no sense a "perfect" economy. It is not a "natural" economy or a self-regulating economy. It is the result of many forces: choices between "more" and "less"; capital costs, labor costs, and organization costs; costs of expansion; costs of research and innovation; costs of security and of trade position. All of these costs and their probable contributions to production and distribution are carefully weighed by managements and decided according to their long-run estimates. There is no predetermined structure or set rule.

It is clear that the assumptions which fitted adequately the classical concept of a natural economy and the assumptions of a managed, mass production and mass distribution economy cannot be bridged over by interpretations, modifications, and prefixes. The assumptions and the analyses of the classical economy must be discarded as inapplicable to the economy of mass production and mass distribution.

The new economy has variously been called "organizational," "corporate," or "managerial." What is needed is a fresh start with theoretical analysis based on facts and practices. The theory should analyze and explain the underlying complexities of the economy. It should point out the difficulties of practical judgment in assessing the benefits and dangers of this economy. Much work of the highest skill has already contributed to this theory. This work needs to be coordinated, so that it can be viewed as a pattern, in spite of its intricacies. Only then can economists with appropriate statistical material apply the tests which the economy must meet. Only then can legal forms and practices be readjusted to produce decisions concerning value that conform to social and economic welfare.

One further caution. The economy of the twentieth century is not homogeneous. It is a mixed economy. About two thirds of it falls under the general heading of mass production and distribution, continuous flow of goods and dynamic change. About one sixth is operated by the government, with methods inconsistently conforming to socialism. The rest (about one sixth) comprises roughly what is included in "small business" and more nearly conforms to the assumptions of classic analysis. These economic systems operate on different principles (side by side) touching each other at many points. We are concerned only with the first, except in so far as the intermingling of the other two adds to the complexity of the economy.

2

SPONTANEOUS GROWTH OF
BUSINESS PRACTICES

THE UNITED STATES ECONOMY is not a simple affair to be described by any title such as "free private enterprise." There is no master blueprint to which business practices must conform. Unlike the great theoretical systems of economics, such as the free-enterprise competition of Adam Smith and his successors, the socialism of Karl Marx, and the cartel system of Europe, the United States economy has taken form through a series of unsystematic adjustments and contrivances designed to cope with situations as they arose. There is planning only in the sense of continual adjustment to a changing set of conditions, different environment, constantly fluctuating values, newly arriving and departing factors. In this respect, the United States government and American business practices stand in sharp contrast to one another, since the Constitution defines in detail the operation of the government.

American business practices have no such defining instrument. The relationship between the network of railroads and its regulation by the ICC; the regulation of public utilities and communications; the varied methods of production, methods of pricing and distribution of the great manufacturing companies; the pricing and production of oil, milk, and coal; the customary "markup" price of many individual retailers and service establishments; price-fixing, "fair" and "unfair" prices; wage rates and conditions of labor; the ethics of professions and businesses; parity prices for basic agricultural products—each has been worked out through discussions, experiments, and relative pressures as a practical solution to a situation.

The result is an exceedingly complex intermeshing of diverse interests, of stages of production and distribution, labor unions, finance, management, customs and established relationships, government laws and regulating agencies, courts and popular opinions.

Trade advantage and bargaining position, in varying degrees of intensity and longevity, permeate every part of the economy. To the outside observer looking in, the control which they generate appears far greater than to the insider looking out.

To the individual exercising this so-called "control," it seems nothing more than influence limited by the basic facts or extraneous forces. Influence sufficient to permit functioning appears essential; insufficient influence cannot prevent the upsurge of chaos; oversufficiency of control may result in oppression to others.

The decade 1890–1900 is perhaps as convenient a period as any other to which to ascribe the beginning of the contemporary shape of the economy. Its origins can be traced even farther back. Its primitive forerunners have always existed, although in a weak and unimportant form. Milling was organized in colonial days. Printing, textiles, shoes, and iron foundries followed in the early years of the republic.

But these first businesses maintained the characteristics of private free enterprise. They were overgrown individuals rather than the institutions which later changed the face of the economy. The managers were a group of individuals rather than a distinctly separate institution.

Such conditions changed only at a slow pace. While the early railroads spanned the gap, they were still largely individualistic. The early history of railroads is associated with such powerful names as Vanderbilt, Gould, Villard, Hill, and Huntington. Later the Harriman system, the Pennsylvania Railroad, the Santa Fe, and the New York Central created institutions. Community enterprises like the Erie Canal bridged an additional gap, but they dominated no more than a local community. They raised problems that were considered exceptional, for the community had no basis for fitting them into the whole.

The great developments which are characterized by the word "revolutionary" can be placed around 1890. By 1910 the movement was well under way; in the twenties it was becoming dominant. Its intermeshing was so devious that it is difficult to pick out any single feature as the deciding characteristic.

Concomitantly, came the preeminence of great banking organizations. The Boston and Philadelphia institutions; and later the New York institutions, with J. P. Morgan as their recognized leader, determined to a large extent the direction of the economy.

Labor organizations followed. The early attempts of the Knights of Labor withered; the American Federation of Labor never attained real power until World War I, and that seeped away during the twenties. Only in the thirties and forties did they establish a powerful trade position.

Agriculture, too, has faced many difficulties in its attempts to free itself of the competitive market and gain an independent trade position. On the whole, cooperative producers' associations have been disappointing. Only when government has intervened, have they achieved temporary security.

Perhaps the first serious break away from the economy of the nineteenth century was due to the growth of specialized machinery and mass production. Machinery could be used only for the purpose in hand. It could not easily be converted to another need. Its value could be recovered only by continued use along the lines intended. The fitful start and stoppage of production dependent on orders was replaced by a flow of production. This flow in turn necessitated a flow of distribution. Systems of marketing had to be devised when the sporadic success of salesmanship fell short of maintaining the flow of production.

Once the flow of distribution was established, many devices for lessening costs of production and increasing usefulness became practicable. Mechanical processes replaced human dexterity, calling for new types of skill and supervision. Regularity of the flow of raw materials and semi-finished parts could be arranged. Labor had to work regular hours to accommodate the flow. The techniques of production at first offered the greatest challenge and induced the keenest intellects to constant efforts. Furnaces operated so uninterruptedly that they retained their heat, thus saving the cost of firing. In glass and pottery making the tunnel replaced the kiln. The kiln required days to put the glass or pottery in place. The product was heated to the required temperature, allowed to cool, and then removed. The tunnel through which it moved automatically heated and cooled according to schedule without loss of time and heat.

Manufacturing productivity per man-hour has increased greatly in recent years; with 100 as a base in 1910, it rose to 289 in 1950 according to Frederick Mills. Other estimates roughly corroborate a tripling of productivity during these years.

These great strides created new problems: labor unrest and a lag in distribution. Long hours of repetitive and exacting work, loss of creative activity by the individual, and irregular employment produced strains. Failure to distribute the flow of products could not be corrected by a simple lowering of price, but required adaptation of the product to an ever widening circle of customers. The professions of "personnel management," "business economics," and "marketing" sprang from these necessities.

Constant improvements in productive efficiency made possible the working day of seven to eight hours and the five-day week. Improved conditions of sanitation, comfort, and safety, greater regularity of employment, removal of petty grievances, pension systems, health and unemployment insurance were determining factors. Standards have been hammered out by labor union leaders and personnel managers in a continuing process of contracts.

The time-honored hierarchy of manufacturer to wholesaler to retailer became more and more limited in scope. Small retailers depending on convenience of location and dealers remaining outside the steady flow of production lessened in importance. Marketing systems take many forms, each adapted to the technique of the product:

1. For heavy machines: exclusive dealers able to service and repair, carrying a stock of spare parts. This is typical of the automobile, harvesting, and refrigerator industries.

2. For specialty articles of occasional use: a limited and

active group of distributors, with appropriate inducements. In the furniture industry each manufacturer concentrates on established outlets—both specialty and department stores. These favored outlets are given special prices during the February and August sales. They are given exclusive rights to certain patterns and first choice of new products. The manufacturer considers that distributors are a part of his organization. His rate of production is so dependent on their selling ability that he employs every method to bind them to him. He attempts to create a permanence analogous to the dealer relationship.

3. For specialties: manufacturers own outlets wherever the demand is sufficient to maintain the establishments. The rubber companies sell partly through their own outlets, partly through exclusive dealers. This results in a situation which may cause competition between themselves and their dealers, and which is considered illegal by the Department of Justice. It might lead to the possibility of a "squeeze" on the dealer.

Yet this situation has grown from the natural reason that not everywhere is the volume sufficient to justify an outlet by the manufacturer. An arrangement that fits one situation does not fit another. Similarly under the Goodyear–Sears Roebuck arrangement, Goodyear was assured a steady and large demand and Sears Roebuck a constant and reliable supply. Sears undertook to buy a fixed annual quantity of tires, and Goodyear undertook to sell at cost-plus instead of at the usual list price minus quantity discounts. This arrangement was freely entered into by both sides because of its desirability for each, but it was declared illegal on the ground that it gave Sears such a price advantage over other distributors, who bought in the established pattern of list prices minus discounts, that it tended to decrease competition. This in practice did not prove to be the case.

4. For standard trade-marked articles of daily use: a system covering all, or as many as possible, distributors. This requires national advertising, price protection, sliding discounts for quantity, quality guaranty, and replacement of unsold articles. Complete coverage is essential, even when loss is suffered; lack of it breaks customer habits, for the margin of advantage is narrow.

Each system has advantages and disadvantages, special inducements, differentials and discriminations. No system is adapted to all articles or all communities. They are similar, however, in that they all mark a departure from price determination through individual bargaining at the market place. The objective of each is to create a steady, uninterrupted flow.

A dissection of distribution discloses many anomalies. Each system favors one customer as against another. Exclusive dealer contracts prevent or discourage others from entering the field. The Supreme Court in cases involving the exclusive filling station contracts of the Standard Oil Company of California held that these contracts, under all the conditions, were violations of Section 3 of the Clayton Act. Subsequently in the Richfield Oil case the Supreme Court sustained a holding that a similar system of contracts violated both the Clayton Act *and* the Sherman Act. However, the Federal Trade Commission has given notice that even under the Clayton Act it does not regard exclusive contracts as illegal *per se*, but that it will apply the rule of reason—or at least *a* rule of reason—to each situation as it arises.

Discount arrangements based on quantity favor the large purchaser. Discount arrangements based on function favor the wholesaler over the retailer, the institutional buyer over either. Degrees of services vary with the requirements of customers. Long-term contracts with fixed quantities and prices are possible for some buyers but not for all. Conditions of payment vary with different credit ratings. Delivery at the factory favors the near-by purchaser. Yet variations of cost are largely subjective estimates.

Moreover, the full product may not be salable at any one price. The same article has different values in different uses. There are narrow alternative choices for one use, perhaps less narrow choices for another. Electric current for home use is more expensive than for factory use. Wheat has a higher value in human consumption than in feed for livestock, yet the demand for bread and crackers is not sufficient to move the entire crop. As a result cheaper grains for livestock are available. It is often impossible to maintain full production together with the same price and uniform conditions. The struggle for survival merges into the struggle for advantageous trade position.

Functional pricing has two meanings. One is in relation to the function of the purchaser—whether secondary manufacturer, wholesaler, or retailer. In this case, the price to the manufacturer is less than the price to the wholesaler and, in turn, the price to the wholesaler is less than the price to the retailer, all regardless of quantity, but only with regard to the purchaser's function in the process of the distribution system. This functional pricing has been challenged by the large retailers, whose quantity purchases are often greater than those of wholesalers.

The other meaning of functional pricing is the purpose

for which the article is used and its differential value in regard to this purpose.

The case of Champion spark plugs describes a situation typical throughout all industry. Champion sold identical spark plugs to automobile manufacturers for use as original equipment, part of the finished motor, for 5 to 7 cents each; and to dealers and wholesalers for resale, for replacement of a worn-out or defective spark plug, for 24 to 27 cents. This practice of functional or differential pricing was questioned by the staff of the Federal Trade Commission on the ground that it was discriminatory.

They maintained that injury to competition was the necessary result, and that the same price should be charged to everyone, no matter to what use the spark plug was to be put. The ensuing hearing disclosed how this practice had developed and how widespread it was throughout industry.

Champion had no system in mind in the development of its functional policy. It faced a situation and adapted its practices to its analysis of advantages and disadvantages.

General Motors and Chrysler made or controlled their own spark plugs. Ford and the minor automobile companies purchased from Champion. These companies had a choice of making their own spark plugs or of buying from any of the forty manufacturers of spark plugs. The advantage to Champion of filling this great mass demand was not only in the lessening of cost through volume, but also in the reputation they attained because so many manufacturers adopted their product. In addition, the close contact with manufacturers enabled Champion to learn accurately their requirements and constantly improve their spark plugs in accord with changing designs. Other makers of spark plugs did not rate these advantages as highly as did Champion, and hence they quoted higher prices to the manufacturers, thus confining themselves to the profitable replacement business.

The Commission ruled that no competition existed between the functions of use as original equipment and use as replacement; hence there could be no injury to competition. However, a differential between purchasers similarly situated was held to be discriminatory and therefore illegal.

A further condition enters into continuous marketing. It is a curious paradox that while stable conditions are highly desirable for the process of maintaining a flow of distribution even with the flow of production, yet improvement of the product, which destroys stability, can also affect marketing favorably. The fixity of demand and supply for which the system is created seldom exists for a length of time. Outside forces are constantly hampering the flow. New products used for the same purpose are offered for sale; new fashions or fads change the direction of consumer purchases; new methods outmode accepted products. The established product is under attack at all times, either in a major sense or through the gnawing away of tiny particles. Stability is not tranquil—it is stability in motion. The rise of the automobile has induced shifts of value and location and habits of living that are little short of sensational. Trucks and airplanes vie with railroads. Rayon, nylon, orlon, and dacron replace silk, linen, even cotton and wool in many uses. Plastics replace rubber, metals, glass, and leather. Farm machinery replaces horses. The economy shifts from peace to war and back again. With all its rigidity, it retains a remarkable flexibility.

So long as minor adjustments can correct an unbalance, an even keel can be maintained by an alert management. But occasionally the innovation is so far-reaching that an entire product or industry is thrown into chaos. When this occurs, a long process of realignment takes place— requiring one or perhaps several years. At worst, salvage is impossible and an entire process or industry shrivels, even disappears. The leather industry, the woolen industry, wither. Sapolio and Pears Soap are happy memories unknown to youth. Powerful trade positions of yesterday are found to be precarious and transient.

All kinds of formal and informal regulatory bodies are set up and devices are invented. The oil industry is controlled by a loose system of state commissions; the men's clothing industry by the decisions of the Amalgamated Clothing Workers. Authoritative statistics of trade associations point out dangers ahead. Government officials sound warnings. Price supports help agriculture. Established trade practices tend to keep the recalcitrants in line. The NRA was but one of many schemes to correct a fundamental unbalance.

The objective of management is not *solely* to achieve a higher rate of production, decreased costs, or higher dividends. It is to maintain a balance in a moving stream of economic forces. And this balance must be an improving balance, or the individual unit will lose its position. A static balance is not enough, for dynamic forces tend to destroy any static situation. Time-honored, sound institutions and methods have their place, but without adaptation to the changing times they shrink in importance and eventually disappear. It is almost as difficult to maintain an old product or institution as it is to introduce and fit a new one into our complex economy. Constant innovations and adaptations underlie the apparent stability of the economic structure. The old institutions survive only because they initiate new methods and ideas. In their search for survival and desire for progress they call in competent experts and accountants to set up a system under which they can continue to operate, and operate more efficiently.

3

THE TOOL OF
ACCOUNTANCY

WHILE THE BEGINNING of accounting may be traced back to the Middle Ages, its evolution was not accelerated until the 1890s. In that decade public accounting acquired firm professional status. Modern accounting originated in England with the creation of the limited-liability company in 1862. Before that time, accounting was mainly concerned with the granting of credit and the conduct of bankruptcy proceedings. Because of the impact of income taxes, the growth of public ownership of corporations, the increased importance of railroad and utility regulation, and the new complexity of the industrial structure, accounting was faced with a succession of more and more difficult problems.

About 1910 the theory and practice of *cost* accounting for use in reviewing costs of manufacturing and direction of effort became widespread. Prominent in this development are the names of Taylor, Count, and Church. This use of cost accounting had a pronounced effect on the evolution of present-day systems of financial and administrative accounting.

The introduction of the income tax in 1913—both corporate and individual—raised many novel questions of theory and interpretation. The increase of these taxes during the war years of 1916–18 brought accounting methods and procedures into startling prominence.

The main concern of accountants today is not with the arithmetic of adding, multiplying, and dividing. This is accomplished by machines. Their concern is with the formulas, postulates, and methods which are most useful in portraying and interpreting the actual situation to persons both inside and outside the company or industry.

Accounting has evolved in conformity with the tremendous changes in the economic pattern. In discussions of accounting there is a tendency to overemphasize the mystery of double entry and to fail to appreciate its conventional character and the limiting effect of its conventions on the significance of its conclusions. All accounting is based on an equation of values. Double entry is merely a technique of analysis, though undoubtedly a very valuable one. The postulates or conventions of the accountants are of a far higher order of importance than the utility of double entry in checking arithmetical accuracy. Accounting evolved from bookkeeping; periodic income reporting evolved from venture accounting.

Business income or profit constitutes the difference between costs of acquisition on the one hand and gross revenue from sale or distribution on the other. Property rights acquired by purchase or production are carried at or below cost; property rights acquired by sales or distribution are carried at the value of the proceeds when the sale is completed. A balance sheet is, therefore, only what its name implies: a statement of balances or equation of values which do not purport to be homogeneous, or simply a summary of the value in terms of cost or market, whichever is lower, of the properties owned, deducting the amounts owed and leading up to a net book value.

Accounting may be approached from four diverse angles —the legal, the individual, the national, and the corporate. The legal angle concerns rate-making by railroads and public utilities, bankruptcy proceedings, income taxes, mergers, and the like. Individual accounting is concerned with measuring the wealth and income of individuals and families, the relative burden of taxes, distribution of income, or the average level of individual welfare as compared to some previous era or to some other community. National accounting concerns itself with aggregate income; its potentiality for war or other great national purposes; the proportion available for investment; the total distribution by classifications such as capital, labor, self-employed. Individual corporate and national accounting together form the raw material of social accounting. These are the aspects of chief interest to economists.

Corporate accounting, with which we are mainly concerned in this study, concentrates on the measuring of income of the three thousand important publicly owned corporations. Violent and increasingly complex changes have followed each other so rapidly that accounting methods adequate at one time have become inadequate under new demands of reporting—SEC requirements, new form of certificates, system reports, and the like. A series of crises has produced landmarks in the development of accounting. Continually revised formulas and new methods have built up the present-day system. This system itself is ever ready to meet new inadequacies as they become manifest. In the course of its evolution, the divergence between financial and administrative accounting has become marked. The aim of *financial* accounting is to present to investors as accurate a picture of the state of the corporation as possible. *Administrative* accounting is devised to enable managements to gauge the past and lay plans for the future.

Accounting is a curious mixture of realism and historic convention, of practical wisdom and theory, of rough adjustment and intricate calculation, of objective standard and subjective estimate. The aim of accounting is not so much to arrive at eternal truth as to present a useful working tool, a guide for judgment.

In this quest, certain postulates are assumed. These postulates are not adopted because they are universally true but because they are useful. The effect of the various postulates must be understood, for they lead to results not necessarily in accord with reality.

1. It is assumed that the value of money is constant. This postulate obviously leads to distortions when the value of money undergoes a great shift; such great shifts are typical of economic history. In appraising any two periods, allowance must be made (either mentally or by calculation based on index numbers) for the effects of these shifts.

2. It is assumed that the corporate institutions which are the main units of accounting are permanent. Through this postulate, accounting does not apply to a series of individual deals or ventures such as the voyage of a trading ship to China, but with the isolation of a period of time out of an indefinite series of past and future periods. Also through this postulate, the estimate of income has become more important than the balance sheet. During the years from 1870 to 1900, the balance sheet was the prime instrument by which estimates of net worth were made. It was the basis for division of income which included in-

vestments and bank loans. It pinpointed value at a certain
time, generally the end of the year. From a comparison
of net worth shown by the balance sheet at the beginning
of the year with that shown at the end of the year, the net
income for the year could be deduced. But, as the complexity of the corporate institution increased, net worth
proved to be inadequate as a guide.

With the emergence of the concept of income as the major determinant of value, the balance sheet has been rele-
gated to a subsidiary place. A postulate of permanence
makes the value of the mass of property rights which have
not reached the disposition stage, but are undergoing constant minute change, almost irrelevant to the measurement of gain, profit, or income.

A single balance sheet does not reveal net worth in
either real or monetary terms. It has become mainly a reference point from which to measure the estimate of income for a specified period. From the balance sheet depreciation and obsolescence are derived; these in turn affect
the estimated income. The balance sheet alone cannot de-
pict the flow of income or its estimate for a given period
of time. It is a static concept in a dynamic economy and
hence a dubious guide for decision or appraisal.

3. It is assumed that no gain takes place until it is realized by sale. The postulate of realization is a useful tool for
the purpose of allocating the period in which a profit (or
loss) has taken place. This is determined by actual sale or
transfer. It is assumed that no change in value occurs until
that moment. Inventory in process of manufacturing has
practical bearings which necessitate separate treatment.
Generally speaking, costs are added to the value as they
are incurred, but profit is not so added. However, in the

case of a finished product which requires years to complete, it is justifiable to include some part of the expected profit. Until the point of actual disposal, the gain or loss is indeterminate.

The postulate fits the facts when production and sale occur in a steady stream. But in the case of irregular production—especially when the time necessary for completion is longer than a year—it yields fitful estimates of income. Its usefulness lies in the fact that it furnishes an objective measure for the period to which gain (or loss) is credited. Its disadvantage lies in that it causes business judgment to be swayed by the effect of taxes. Exceptions to this postulate are made when it obviously distorts the picture too violently.

The realization of gain (and tax) can often be avoided by not selling. Losses previously incurred can be realized for the purpose of offsetting gains. The actual tax accordingly may have little relation to the gain that actually occurred during a period.

It has been said that these postulates are to be judged by their utility rather than by their truth. Indeed, they are necessary, for they furnish the basis on which the accountant can make a report. They enable him to make decisions according to "accepted principles" of accounting.

Accountants may be divided into two schools of thought. One holds that the accountant should take the lead in setting up a series of corrections which more truly closes the gap between the postulates and the facts. This would involve such matters as index numbers to be applied to depreciation, capital values, and inventory. Together with management, he would accept full responsibility for subjective estimates. He would make his statements suitable for the purpose in mind without further interpretation. The logic behind this position is that only the accountant and the management are in full possession of all the facts and therefore are best able to evaluate them. The accountant following this policy would assume the attitude of an umpire.

The second school of thought holds that the accountant is not concerned with interpretation, but only with certifying the correctness of the report made by the management. He should state the principles used, so that the reader may know exactly the postulates involved and be enabled to make his own interpretation. With full disclosure the accountant's responsibility ceases. He clings to accepted standards, on the grounds that corrections involve an estimate (or guess) of the future course of prices, taxes, or sales and that, in any event, depreciation and new investment are sufficiently rapid to keep the inaccuracy of the published statements within reasonable bounds. The accountant who adopts this position would assume the attitude of scorekeeper. This point of view throws the burden of analysis on the reader, so that the interpretation of accounts has called into being a new profession of investment analysis.

The postulate of the stability of the monetary unit represents a distortion of both the balance sheet and income statement in a period of changing price level, either up or down. Taken from decade to decade, the general price level has varied as much as 25 to 30 percent, either up or down. The decade prior to 1896 saw a fall in the price level; then came a rise until 1907; this was followed by a fall until World War I. A violent rise during the war was followed by the sharpest drop on record and then a decade of relative stability in the twenties. The thirties saw a sharp drop, followed in the forties by a slight rise during World War II and a violent rise from 1945 to 1952. As a result, the costs incurred for similar objects vary greatly, depending on whether they are current costs or costs of one, ten, or twenty years past. The balance sheet and the income statement are both distorted by this situation. As shown in the report on "Changing Concepts of Business Income," accountants differ in regard to the best methods to be employed.

A similar discrepancy is found in the variety of methods used for evaluation of inventory—by cost or market value (whichever is lower); through the last-in first-out method (LIFO) based on a selected moment of time; by average price over a series of years. The change in the price level applicable to inventory (about a year) is not so great as is likely in an investment which may have been made years ago.

Nevertheless, when the gain or loss of inventory value is added to the operating income, the total imputed to any period by cost or market value differs greatly from the imputed income of LIFO. Companies differing in their methods cannot be compared. Differences in the estimate of profit of 10 to 20 percent are common, and they may be even greater.

Every corporation carries a fringe of investments no longer useful in operation. Items such as an abandoned warehouse, a factory, a plot of ground, or an unused mine are for a period carried at their cost price. When any one of such items is sold, the profit or loss is stated in accord with the postulates of realization.

The timing of the sale in relation to profits or losses realized in other transactions is more important than the price, especially under an excess profits tax. In such cases the postulate of realization is used to distort rather than to clarify. To have an inflated balance sheet value, based on the current price level, is a tax asset.

The postulate of permanence requires the maintenance of the physical capital necessary for production. This, in turn, calls not only for maintenance of equipment, but also for a depreciation charge to care for replacement. The method of charging depreciation has a confused history, largely due to its application to public utility accounting, where the theory of permanence was first applied. The view is widely held that depreciation is an arbitrary allocation of costs over a specified period, unrelated to the replacement cost of the capital value. Depreciation is therefore not theoretical, but opportunistic—a convenient method of charging relatively permanent portions of manufacturing costs over a period of time. However objective the method used for estimating the life of any capital item, this is a subjective estimate. Of necessity, it is an overstatement or understatement of the years of use which lie ahead. That can only be known after the event, not in advance. Whether depreciation over the years is taken at a decelerated rate or at an even rate has a tremendous effect on the flow of estimated income. In the first case it reduces the estimate for the early years and increases the estimate for the later years. In the second case it has the opposite effect. The decisions of the United States Department of the Treasury during the 1940s tended toward the use of the straight-line method, for this increased tax revenues in the years immediately ahead. The use of depreciation in public statements permitted by the Treasury

Department tends to overstate the income which is relied upon to determine value.

The income tax law of 1953 widened the discretion of management in determining depreciation. The depreciation over a five-year period for new construction, which was permitted on a certificate of necessity issued by the Department of Defense, tended to increase the annual depreciation charge; thus decreasing the resultant income and the taxes based upon it.

An ingenious method of increasing depreciation charges is the so-called lease-back sale. This is how it works in practice. If a manufacturer builds a new structure for $1 million, he will usually write off depreciation over twenty-five years—$40,000 per year. But, by selling this building to an investor at cost, he can arrange rentals at a much higher figure during the early years and at a nominal rate after the original cost plus interest has been returned. The rental may be $200,000 per year (plus interest) for five years and after that $10,000 or option to buy at a low figure. The investor gets his money back and the manufacturer pays lower taxes, so both are satisfied at the expense of the Treasury Department. This is indeed a saving under two conditions: that the depreciation allowed by the Treasury Department is less than the facts warrant, or that the tax rates will turn out to be less after the period of high rental—in this case five years. The stipulated rental replaces the compulsory rate of depreciation, thus affecting both costs and estimated income.

In a rapidly changing industrial technique, obsolescence occurs sooner than the physical wearing out of equipment, causing unforeseen losses. Moreover, depreciation is limited to the dollar cost of each item, which in a period of rising prices is insufficient for replacement. Conversely, in a period of falling prices, it is more than sufficient. Complex problems are introduced by the fact that seldom, if ever, is any piece of equipment replaced by its exact duplicate. The railroad flatcar was the classic example of changelessness. Even this seems to be evolving new forms because of innovations in loading techniques. Universally, new equipment is streamlined and has a modern design, which makes for more efficiency. Perhaps an entirely new technique has been introduced. In a dynamic economy, no management can stand still for any length of time without losing its position.

Quite apart from depreciation, obsolescence brings about reduced value of investment. Its recognition in an accounting system on a regular basis introduces many elements of judgment that are insusceptible of proof. An interesting illustration of this is the experience of the United States Steel Corporation as explained in its annual reports of 1935 and 1948.

This cannot be better described than in the language of the reports themselves. The 1935 report stated:

There was completed during the year a detailed analysis of the investment in depreciable property, which, as stated in the annual report for 1934 had been undertaken by the subsidiary companies. This analysis resulted in adjustments of the Property Investment account effecting a reduction of net book values. Broadly, these adjustments are attributable to the developments in the art and mechanics of steel-making which have operated to reduce the normally expected life of such facilities, and to changes in plant location based upon shifting markets and transportation facilities. The factors involving present or prospective abandonments of obsolete units, from time to time, impose unusual depreciation charges which the property survey has attempted to record as reflecting present conditions. The above adjustment, amounting to a net of $88,720,028.04, has been effected by transferring that amount from the Surplus account termed "Appropriated for and Invested in Capital Expenditures," which heretofore was carried at $270,000,000. The remainder of the account, $181,- 279, 971.96, has been transferred to and converted into a general reserve for amortization of property investment valuation.

In view of the fact that the surplus account appropriated for and invested in Capital Expenditures was invested in fixed property, it was considered advisable that the adjustment and transfer as described should be made as indicated. Capital investment expenditures to the amount of $181,279,971.96 having heretofore been financed specifically by such segregated surplus account, it follows that future depreciation allowance should not be made therefor in reporting consolidated net income. This reduction in annual depreciation allowances, will, however, be offset, in part at least, by increased allowances in calculated future depreciation charges which will result from the revised depreciation rates indicated by the analysis above mentioned.

The gross Property Investment Account, inclusive of Intangibles, as shown in table . . . and as carried in the consolidated balance sheet, is based on the amount of capital stock and bonds of the Corporation issued for the acquirement of the subsidiary companies and cash, plus cash expenditures made for additional property acquired since the organization of the Corporation and less (a) the sum of $508,302,500, heretofore written off for Intangible values which was provided from Earned Surplus, and (b) credits for investment value of property sold, retired or otherwise disposed of. . . . the balance of the reserves provided from income and surplus for accrued depletion, depreciation, obsolescence and amortization of the present gross investment in plant and property amounts at December 31, 1935, to an aggregate of $1,124,107,-707.52. These reserves include the adjustments of $88,720,-028.04, and the transfer of the $181,279,971.96 mentioned in the preceding paragraphs.

However, by 1948 the situation had changed, and the capital write-off was restored. In the report for that year it was stated:

In 1935, following a detailed analysis of the Corporation's investment in properties, $270 million was added, by action of the Board of Directors, to the depreciation reserves to cover economic obsolescence of these properties. This amount had been reserved prior to 1927, principally from earned surplus, as management's estimate of the amount of income which had been reinvested in machinery, plants and mines. When this additional depreciation reserve was set up in 1935, the steel-making subsidiaries had operated for five years at an average of less than one third of capacity and property prices were substantially lower than in the preceding decade. This addition to the depreciation reserves was for the purpose of stating conservatively the net property values based on then existing economic conditions. The economic situation has been so altered by World War II and what has followed that this reserve, in the opinion of the Board of Directors, is no longer needed for the purposes anticipated in 1935. Therefore the Board of Directors has authorized that this amount of $270 million, no part of which has ever been treated as a depreciation cost in income statements or allowed as a deduction for income tax purposes, be transferred back to earned surplus from depreciation reserves, effective as of December 31, 1948.

The two corrections are almost unique in the practice of corporate accounting. Closely parallel was an adjustment made by the Imperial Chemical Company. In the annual report of 1950 it was stated: "It must be pointed out that depreciation calculated and charged in this manner, although it will suffice to write off the manufacturing assets over their remaining lives, will still fail to provide in full against the total cost of replacing those assets when the time for replacement arises." Accordingly, an extra £5 million was charged to Obsolescence and Replacement of Assets. The report continued: "In other words, the valuation is that of the estimated present-day costs of construction or acquisition of the Company's manufacturing assets reduced to take account of the age of the assets—not the full cost of the present-day replacement of such assets in new conditions."

Consequently capital reserves were raised from about £17 million to about £118 million, increasing depreciation from £6,600,000 to £8,700,000.

A new principle permitting "accelerated depreciation" over a five-year period was introduced by the United States government in order to speed up war and later defense production. The logic of this was that the value of the equipment would have depreciated through the reduction of demand when the emergency was over. The permission to charge off this accelerated depreciation tended to understate the estimated income during those five years, *if* the demand justified. The value of the equipment rather than its physical condition was the determinant. This was scarcely an informed estimate: it was a subjective guess. It led to different depreciation rates for similar machines used side by side.

Perhaps the best theoretical definition of depreciation would be: that amount charged off which exactly maintains the earning power of capital in relation to technical change and to competition, including a reduction of the

useful life of the property. Granted the accuracy of the
definition, this is indeed a difficult evaluation when confined to any year. Such a standard would be a highly subjective estimate, with variations year by year depending
on internal and external factors. The difficulty of computa-
tion is itself sufficient to reject it as a working hypothesis.
Straight-line depreciation has the virtue of simplicity and
exactness.

It appears that the wide variety of industrial techniques
and methods precludes any single system of accounting
from portraying accurately the situation to those not acquainted with the peculiarities of the industry.

To sum up, the accountant is not, as many consider him,
a master of dexterity with figures. Accuracy in the footing
of columns of figures, in multiplying and dividing does
not play as large a part in his life as is believed. The arithmetical part of accounting is done by machines. The accountant is, or should be, a philosopher who ponders over
the principles by which he can most correctly portray the
situation so that the wisdom of the decisions of many people who have no access to the intimate facts is not be-
trayed. He confers with lawyers, legislators, and administrative officials over the principles which will best serve
purposes of investment, rate-making, taxation, direction
of expansion, and any other purposes for which accounts
are used. The interpretation of these principles in the
great variety of practical situations presented by the techniques of different industries is of absorbing interest and
financial importance. Disaster or success follows the mis-
understanding or understanding of financial statements. In
this case, how can anyone suppose that "profit" or "loss"
is so exact a figure that any business executive can make

the precise calculations required to "maximize profit" on the sale of any single article? Yet this concept forms the basis of the traditional economic theory.

Of late, accountants have assumed a new function. The extraordinarily rapid growth of mechanical devices has transformed the very nature of accounting to a degree comparable to the developments of the production line in industry. This has had repercussions on business practices far beyond the narrow bounds of the accounting profession.

The lessened cost of record-keeping has opened new possibilities of small accounts in banking, and it has made almost instantaneous the reporting of transactions by branches to the main office, thus rendering centralized control far more effective. This has been an influence inducing bank mergers, which gain the advantages of large capital accumulation with the convenience of many scattered branches.

Similarly, this speeding up of intercommunication makes more effective the branching out of retail stores, accelerating the tendency toward chains, as opposed to small independent operations.

Manufacturing concerns are helped through the quickened control over their supplies and operations. The multiple parts entering into assembly are more effectively controlled if each is a part of the whole rather than made by independents and sold to the assembler. Vertical unification is thus encouraged.

The increased complexity of the corporate tax structure has impelled accountants to enter into—indeed to control to a high degree—the determination of the amount of the income tax. The erosion of the uniform levy has taken place through the granting of a stream of exceptions. If the oil industry is granted an exemption for depletion, why should this not be extended to the mining industry for depletion of coal, iron ore, copper, lead, zinc, and the many specialized ores? From there it is only a step to clay, kaolin, and crushed rock. Exceptions are so numerous that a specialist is required to keep track of them and to take advantage of individual or group situations.

The immunities extended to inventors, writers of novels, painters, and others are demanded by professional athletes, doctors, and those whose high earnings are concentrated in one year or in a limited number of years, though their work at unremunerative returns may extend over a long period.

The wide extension of pension funds creates new problems of allocation of income to specific years. These are measured by arbitrary formulas beyond the ability of any but a specialist to compute. Furthermore they create the anomaly of being regarded as an expense by a corporation while no such privilege is accorded to an individual.

The high rate of taxes involves more than a difference in degree or new techniques. It creates a new situation involving a basic change. The dividing line between the accounting profession and the legal profession becomes blurred, requiring a new formula hammered out by a committee representing both professions. Just as the original advertising agency has evolved into a market research organization, so accountants' new services to their customers result in widespread effects on the pattern of business structure. The accountant's services in helping organizations to establish a firm trade position by reorganizing their entire financial systems are of inestimable value.

4

THE TRADE POSITION OF
INDUSTRY

ADVANTAGEOUS TRADE POSITION of differing degrees of magnitude, extent, and longevity is typical of industrial corporations and is almost their cornerstone. The cases are rare and diminishing in which supply and demand of the market place, devoid of any other influence, determine price. So general is the influence of trade position that it might well be shown that the success of any economic group or enterprise depends on its proper and skillful use, while avoiding its abuse. For abuse leads to its termination. Judgment is required to determine the limits of control of a trade position.

There are many varieties of trade positions, each based on possession of a definite asset. Sometimes they supplement each other; at other times they seem to counteract or neutralize each other. Because advantages which constitute a trade position cannot be measured in any exact sense, they are generally not included in the balance sheet. But they can be, and are, assessed in various ways. Their total value shows up in the net result of operation. It is evaluated when shares are bought and sold.

No concern can have every trade advantage. Hence the choice of which particular trade advantage to pursue and which is most possible to attain in each particular situation is of the utmost importance.

ADVANTAGE OF LOCATION

Widespread advantage, of a limited degree, is based on locality. A small community may have but one of a kind of a great variety of tradesmen and service establishments. In the community, within the limits of convenience to the nearest large center of population, each of these tradesmen and establishments controls the excellence of product, the price and service. Any local distributor or service station has the advantage of naming his terms and prices, depending on the inconvenience of getting the same article or service at a distance. It is a species of negative nuisance value. This may be trivial or important. The slogans "patronize local trade" or "home owned" capitalize on community solidarity. They have a definite appeal, as outsiders invading a community, especially the chain stores, have discovered to their sorrow.

Petty advantage, due to locality, is apt to remain undisturbed. The local barber, the local contractor, the local banker in a small community, in fact all the sole purveyors of local services, have an advantage due to the difficulty of dealing with more distant purveyors of the same service. They are not normally circumscribed by local ordinances. The taxicab company or the garbage collector is more likely to come under supervision.

Strategic locations can be placed in this classification, notably the spaces in railroad stations, hotels, and similar public places. The American News Company locations come conspicuously in this category. They seek to supply the entirety of whatever demand there is. Access to rail or port facilities may at times be important, but in general these are available in quantity beyond the requirements.

Advantage based on locality can be extended beyond its original nuisance value. Local plumbers can band together to install and service only the brands which they carry, so that a manufacturer without a local dealer and service agent finds it impossible to sell his bathroom or toilet fixtures. This condition has seriously impeded the sale of Sears Roebuck bathroom and plumbing products. Labor unions have insisted that stone should be cut and polished on the spot where a building is being erected, instead of at the quarry; this in spite of the fact that the work could be done more cheaply and efficiently at the quarry where the equipment and organization are superior. Building regulations are drawn up to hamper and even exclude products from outside the favored area.

Similarly important, though for different reasons, is the advantage of location for factories. Availability of transportation, either by rail, water, or truck; proximity of raw material or of markets; an adequate labor supply; rates of taxation—all play their part. Abundant forests first drew the furniture industry to Michigan. When the forests were depleted and wood was brought from a distance, the existence of a trained working force kept the industry there. An ample supply of pure water, as in Fernandina, Florida, determines the location of Celanese plants. The steel industry moves from one location to another as the availability of iron and coal varies. Gary, Indiana, is reported to have outstripped Pittsburgh in tonnage; the Delaware River area is accessible to iron shipments by sea and hence is expanding with the aid of seaborne ore.

While location is an important trade advantage, it is not

conclusive. Other advantages are often more important. Moreover, the value of location is ephemeral. Trading areas move; transport facilities change; raw materials become less available; new raw materials are discovered. A more static influence in the economy is the trained and skilled working force. Family homes and accustomed neighborhoods can be moved only under terrific pressure. The resistance in New England is startling, but it has finally yielded to new techniques.

The advantage of an isolated location contrasts sharply with the situation where two restaurants, moving picture theaters, or leading stores are side by side, thus creating an area or neighborhood. It is considered that the joint drawing power is so much greater than that of either one singly that they supplement, rather than harm each other. The isolation of Wanamaker's in New York on 9th Street was a general trade disadvantage, in contrast to its convenience for the population in the immediate vicinity, and led ultimately to the closing of the store. The 34th Street and the upper Fifth Avenue areas have the magnetism of many individual units which supplement each other. Theaters in New York are grouped together, for the most part near Broadway between 44th and 50th Streets. This situation may change with the movement of population. Suburban shopping centers are planned in advance as a magnet to attract customers. Downtown areas for shoppers are roughly limited, so that within a small space a decided advantage accrues as compared with adjacent blocks. Chain stores have elaborate systems for determining the comparative value of sites.

ADVANTAGE OF EXCLUSIVE POSITION

There are many occasions where a person or business concern dominates a field which is so limited that it could not support more than one organization—a fact so clearly recognized that it is not worth while for a potential competitor to emerge. Such a situation is exemplified by an importer of an article of minor importance; an agent for a small country; a specialist in a less important branch of law or medicine; the sole agent (whether or not exclusive) of a manufacturer. The automobile, farm implement, or refrigerator manufacturer has one dealer in a small community, granting him exclusive rights and protecting his rights within a given territory. This is often necessary, for without it the dealer could not contemplate investing the required overhead. In metropolitan centers such exclusive rights are less necessary.

Such a trade position is at best of only minor importance. Should it become important there would be little to prevent a competitor from entering the field.

ADVANTAGE OF CUSTOM

Individuals in a group or profession gain an advantage through the adoption of a code of ethics or customs which tends to perpetuate existing relationship with suppliers or customers. This is the kind of advantage which the Department of Justice accused investment bankers of exploiting. Judge Medina's decision that the practice under attack was a normal and necessary outgrowth is in line with the point of view developed here.

The charge was that investment bankers did not compete actively for new issues of companies which had always made use of a particular investment firm. Such a lack of competition was alleged to be tantamount to an agreement not to invade another's territory, and hence tended toward monopoly. Each firm had a limited trade position in its own special field, amounting to decided advantage. Together they covered almost the entire activity, so that there was said to be no market place except in respect to new companies which needed financing. Yet even here challenge has come from the outside. Insurance companies have directly purchased new issues of securities. The proportion of the total new issues taken by insurance companies, according to Judge Medina, rose from 14 percent in 1936 to 72 percent in 1948.

Aside from the legal aspects and arguments, the economic problems involved in this case are (1) whether trade position is a necessary feature of the requirement for a certain degree of orderliness; and (2) whether the advantages of intimate association outweigh the possible lower costs of the market place. Such intimate association requires the investment company to supply help in time of trouble, reliable advice, and discussion of major policies, especially in regard to finance and choice of securities to be issued. None of these are available through the competitive sealed bids of the market place.

Respect for each other's clients is customary among doctors; it is less so among lawyers and engineers; it is totally lacking among merchants and construction promoters. The established practice of a lawyer or doctor is based on the fact that he has cumulative knowledge (sometimes very long and very intimate) of his client, and that consequently the client naturally finds it easier to turn to him as the need arises. The sheer labor and expense of becoming familiar with the detailed history of the client gives an enormous edge to the individual or firm which already has this knowledge through years of association. Slight preference is not enough to force a change; the dissatisfaction (or need) must be great.

In the case of accountants, there is much to be argued in favor of a change every year or periodically. Yet again, the local knowledge is so great and its acquisition so time-consuming that rarely does any concern feel itself justified in incurring the expense involved. Therefore, instead of changing accounting firms each year, clients request that partners and senior accountants in charge of their audits be alternated in order to get a new point of view. Thus collusion, setting up false inventories, and other pitfalls which every accountant faces may be detected more easily. At the same time, the accounting firm familiar with the client's financial status can be retained.

In every case of professional advantage the fear of loss of this advantage is a more potent factor than would appear to the outsider looking in. Once a client is lost, he is gone forever. And it is more difficult to find a new client than to hold an old one, hence emphasis is placed upon preserving established relationships. Failure to deliver develops an irritation that weakens and finally snaps the bonds. Such established relationships are not eternal, though they might appear so to an outsider. There is more underground seeping away than appears on the surface.

ADVANTAGE OF REPUTATION

An established reputation may be the source of considerable and prolonged advantage. Indeed, so necessary is reputation to many individuals and organizations that it is safeguarded by expensive practices and cumbersome rules.

In the case of branded and trade-marked articles, the established quality is expected to lead satisfied consumers to specify the brand in repurchasing. In the case of canned or packaged foods, which must of necessity be purchased without test and unseen, the only guide for the consumer is previous knowledge of the satisfaction given. Variation is attended by great risk. Even a suspicion of deteriorated quality by the consumer may cause him to turn to another brand. Dissatisfaction on the part of relatively few consumers will sometimes plunge the manufacturer down the scale. Any loss of sales is accompanied by increased overhead per unit. Once a certain reputation is established, it must be maintained to prevent experimentation on the part of the consumer. On the other hand, a superior product without reputation faces many difficulties in persuading consumers to change. Until it is known to be superior, great costs of carrying charges have been incurred and much time consumed.

Such continuity of quality becomes exceedingly difficult to maintain in view of the changes in the quality of raw products and in their prices, particularly when the finished product is a compound. The excellence of many crops varies from year to year with rainfall, drought, storm, and sunshine. The tomato crop in California is so inferior in some years that many canneries drop this item entirely from their line rather than risk criticism. The price of cocoa and coffee beans has varied greatly in recent years; yet the price of the finished product can follow only slowly the varying costs. The finished product—sold in can or package—must maintain a standard, or reputation is imperiled.

The change in cost of the raw product is often so great that the consumer would balk at a similar change in the finished product. Likewise, he would balk at a reduction of quality or quantity. The manufacturer is faced with the alternative of losing his reputation or supplying his product at a loss. One or another of the many lines of the General Foods Corporation is normally sold for a prolonged period at a reduced profit, or none, or perhaps at a loss. If the loss is temporary, no great importance is attached to it. But it *may* be prolonged or permanent. In contrast, a loss of reputation—and the trade advantage that accompanies it—is *sure* to be prolonged, if not permanent.

Reputation is necessarily exclusive. Reputation for everything is impossible. One firm can have a reputation for impeccability, another for smartness, another for low price and good values. Each has a trade position of limited but very real worth. Reputation may be country-wide, as in the case of Wrigley's gum or Gillette razors, Campbell's soups or Ivory soap; or it may be limited to a small group of customers or to a single city.

General Foods Corporation elects to minimize its general connection with all of its brands, preferring to have each earn its own position. In contrast, General Motors, General Electric, S & W Fine Foods, Del Monte, and others emphasize their sponsorship of each of their products, expecting their general reputation to guarantee each. Reputation may at times be carried over from one area to another. It is a difficult process, and one not necessarily successful.

ADVANTAGE OF ESTABLISHED ORGANIZATION

Established organization is a major advantage. A complete organization has many ways of using its accumulated skills denied to a partial organization. Once established, it can offer unique articles and services. An organization is difficult and expensive to create, in terms of both time and money. The potential rival who starts from scratch must count on heavy expenses, losses, and inefficiency while the process of learning is under way.

The classic example is ALCOA, as described by Judge Learned Hand:

It was not inevitable that it should always anticipate increases in the demand for ingot and be prepared to supply them. Nothing compelled it to keep doubling and redoubling its capacity before others entered the field. It insists that it never excluded competitors; but we can think of no more effective exclusion than progressively to embrace each new opportunity as it opened, and to face every newcomer with new capacity already geared into a great organization, having the advantage of experience, trade connections and the elite of personnel.

Another instance of trade position through organization that verges on permanence is the dominant department store in a medium-sized metropolis. Such a store does half the volume of available business—about as much as all other comparable stores together. In consequence, it has a buying, management, and sales organization beyond the reach of any others. It has a breadth and depth of selection that no other can approach. It could not have attained this position without a broad good will in all classes of the community. Any potential rival who might strive for a similar organization would bankrupt himself in the process. In view of his smaller clientele he could not possibly rival the range of selection. Articles demanded only occasionally would gather dust unless they were exposed to a great stream of customers. Yet without such articles the great stream would never come into existence. On the other hand, such a position is constantly subject to external attrition. A specialty store might take some of its customers in its limited field. Chain stores with less service and less expense may nibble at it by attracting a certain amount of trade. Stores located in suburban areas for convenience have a limited drawing power.

Such dominant establishments are difficult to create and require many years—even generations—to attain their maturity. They depend on deep-rooted habits. They are rare; there are not more than a half dozen that indisputably could be included in this classification. It is more usual that the largest is followed closely enough by two or three so that the advantages are not preponderant. At times, in spite of the dominance of one organization, the specialty and chain stores are so developed that the advantage is slight.

Parallel to this organization in the retail field is the advantage in a territory of the organized sales force of a manufacturer. The invasion of new territory by a drug concern means far more than the sending of salesmen with samples. It entails the warehousing of sufficient stock for replacement, the building up of a sufficient volume to keep fresh goods always on the counter, the attempt to create through advertising and related publicity a changed habit of buying by potential consumers. The process is expensive in time and money and not assured of success. Stocks of merchandise must be carried even though demand is small. This results in deterioration, clearance, and loss. Samples are given out freely—left in doorways or distributed through restaurants.

The introduction of English automobiles in the United

States—no matter how excellent—is hampered by lack of expert repairmen and delay in procuring spare parts. The same is true of the smaller American motor companies. Foreign made sewing machines and typewriters present a similar problem. The new company is faced by an established network of experienced men who can give prompt service of the highest order.

An unexpected example of established organization is the case of cotton sheet manufacturers. In spite of the high degree of likeness among sheets it has proved so difficult to break into established habits that certain cities are known in the trade as the property of certain brands. For a long period one brand was predominant in San Francisco (indeed on the Pacific Coast) and in Cleveland; another equally so in St. Louis, Missouri, and the adjacent territory; another in Scranton, Rochester, Buffalo, Syracuse, and neighboring cities; and yet another in Pittsburgh and Youngstown. Efforts to break into any of these territories had to be accompanied by costly advertising allowances and special discounts, and even then they were singularly unsuccessful. Dealers could not afford to carry stocks of sheets which they could not sell.

In each case the original advantage seems to date back to a particularly energetic agent in a certain city who managed to create a demand so great that momentum has carried it on for many years. Of late, the advantage has apparently dwindled. Cannon Mills broke through by offering percale sheets for the price of muslin. Springs Mills established a position through a tremendously clever advertising campaign. The national situation has eaten into local prejudice.

The building of an organization is a slow and difficult

process. As a rule the best known men are not available. Choice has to be made among those who can be found, some of whom will surely prove incompetent. That means replacement and delay. Men and women must get acquainted with one another and learn to speak a common language. They must learn to know their resources and their customers. They can only slowly reach reliable judgments of what is possible and what is futile. Expansion is impossible unless the organization is already capable of conducting its operations. Therein lies the paradox: a new project cannot be launched without an adequate organization, yet the building of the organization cannot be accomplished in a vacuum. It must grow by a series of steps, and be allowed to jell during certain selected intervals before it is required to undertake new projects.

Inevitably, errors of judgment are more frequent in the new than in the established organization. Good judgment is not applied in a generalization but in specific cases. The advantageous situation which the new organization seeks to exploit must be sufficiently great and permanent to overcome the obstacles of immaturity. It must have sufficient financial backing to withstand a period of losses—perhaps prolonged. Hence it is always more possible to launch an offshoot of an existing organization than to start from scratch. At least some parts of the offshoot are already familiar, and the rest can be developed.

This is exactly what occurs. Most development is from an already established base. A copper company produces molybdenum, nickel, lead, or aluminum; an oil company expands into related plastics; a rubber company develops synthetic rubber and may even manufacture chemicals. The sharp division between industries becomes blurred, so that "interindustry" competition becomes many sided, no longer clear cut. Analysis becomes confused; attempts to mold industry into a convenient pattern are difficult, as will be developed later.

Even a poor organization can more easily be improved than a new one created; however, improvement also has its difficulties. When an existing organization is shifted from low gear to high gear there are many individuals who simply cannot respond to the new order. Not that they are unwilling; they are incapable. Custom and personal abilities have fitted them into the old order. They cannot adapt themselves. Yet the confusion of too many changes also plays havoc.

In the reorganization of a moribund concern dilemmas arise from which there is no escape. Either slow introduction of small quantities of new blood proves so highly irritant to the majority that frustration develops, or the rapid injection of new blood causes the character of the whole to undergo a change and thus leads to confusion and loss of morale over a considerable period of time. In any case, it is a lengthy, painful, and costly process.

The life span of any management is about twenty or twenty-five years. After that, settled habits and the viewpoint of the past have it in their grip. New blood must constantly be introduced. This is difficult, however, for the prestige of yesterday's success carries over. The new blood may turn out to be less wise than was hoped. Family concerns are especially vulnerable to deterioration. Others in which choice was free have also had unfortunate experiences. Not infrequently, a key executive fails to fit into a new environment, and is eased out after a short period. Top management has no primrose bordered road.

But within these limits an organization that is both stable and dynamic, geared to accomplish its field of purpose, has a trade advantage of enormous proportion.

ADVANTAGE OF RESOURCE OWNERSHIP

Sole ownership of a natural resource is rare. This is one of the few cases to which the word "monopoly" can properly be applied. Conspicuous examples are the International Nickel Company and, at one time, the Aluminum Company of America. Control of bauxite was only the beginning and did not last long. More important were patents and organization. The ownership of many minor metals approaches practical monopoly. Whatever restraints on their operation remain come from the alternative use of other metals. Possibility of this is a matter of technique, and varies greatly in different situations. Aluminum and nickel have almost unique qualities for many purposes. But neither could exist *solely* on the exploitation of its unique advantages. In order to broaden output they must enter the arena where they have relatively small advantage. This necessitates a lower price than could have been dictated by the most favorable situation. Users are constantly experimenting in alternate metals and methods. The advantage appears greater to the outsider than to the insider.

In the oil industry, the integrated company has a great advantage over the single operational company. Each company has as its goal the production of a large share of its crude oil rather than the purchase of it. At least 50 percent is considered desirable, and more if possible. This control makes possible smoother operation of its refineries.

Taken as a whole, the ratio of increase of the proven reserves of oil to production is 1½ to 1.

In the steel industry, ownership of coal and iron ore is essential. A frequently used basis is that forty years of supply must be maintained. With the depletion of the ore of the Mesabi Range, great projects to develop new sources in Canada, Venezuela, and even more distant territories were undertaken.

In the lumber industry, no large sawmill could operate on purchased timber. The Weyerhaeuser Company, for example, has a policy of replacing its annual production by new planting.

ADVANTAGE OF FEW COMPETITORS

Trade advantage through oligopoly may at times be considerable, especially when combined with trade ethics, codes, and customs. A small group can in many ways more easily adopt like methods favorable to the industry as a whole than would be possible in a larger group.

Oligopoly is itself a vague term. How many are few? A frequently adopted number is four, and it is found what percentage of the total volume is marketed by these four. Perhaps this vagueness should be included in its definition, "Such a number as are capable of being organized in such a manner as to create joint power." That might include the seventeen investment bankers, if it had been found that their ethics and codes resulted in ability to regulate conditions to their own advantage. It was also alleged by the economists of the Federal Trade Commission that sixty-three dealers in motor tires, constituting 0.131 percent of all dealers (48,198) had such an advantage over the others through their larger discounts as to justify a complaint. Are sixty-three so few as to constitute an oligopoly? Use of the term oligopoly involves, therefore, a questionable judgment as to what fewness is and whether fewness creates unreasonable advantage.

So much is certainly true, even if it does not justify the extreme judgment that oligopoly is indistinguishable in its results from true monopoly. Opinions differ strongly on this point, especially when carried on in terms of black (monopoly) and white (competition). But in terms of some degree of trade advantage, oligopoly, as compared to many units in an industry, would seem to qualify.

A different view of oligopoly is taken here as more realistic. This view maintains that only in oligopoly (as opposed to many small units) can completeness of market knowledge on the part of the consumer exist which is required for careful selection. Purchasers cannot possibly understand the entire market for a nonstandardized article provided by an infinitude of sellers, so that many transactions are consummated in ignorance of other opportunities. On the other hand, only when the number of manufacturers is limited is close comparison of performance and price feasible.

In this view of oligopoly, competition for trade advantage is at its keenest. Each producer watches the other. Each struggles for an enhancement of its total share of the market. Each is capable of looking after itself and of adopting any new method or of creating any new product innovated by another. Each has an established core of demand and looks for its gains by increasing hold on the fringe demand. Actual control is far more difficult than the structure of the industry would indicate.

Moreover, there is the constant attempt of a neighboring industry to overstep the borders of its original enterprise. A copper company develops aluminum, and then is followed immediately into the new field by its rivals. General Motors manufactures road-making machinery and Diesel engines; Continental Can Company makes paper milk containers in rivalry with companies making glass bottles. It is always possible for a large motor company to build its own tires instead of buying from one of the rubber companies. General Motors makes its own spark plugs, whereas Ford buys from Champion. The degree of ease of entry is a strong limitation on oligopolistic control. Federated Department Stores reaches into small communities by creating, at one stroke, under the title of Fedway, eight stores of dominant size in as many communities.

ADVANTAGE OF BIGNESS

While oligopoly and bigness have some relation to each other, bigness, as such, is an unquestioned and major source of advantage. Vague as the definition of bigness is, yet under any definition in a quantitative or qualitative sense, considerable ability to adjust terms and to name conditions is present. This ability has led to a confused series of governmental limitations, either by acts of Congress, by consent decree, or by court order.

The court history of bigness is varied. It has been held of no importance, and it has been held a cause for dissolution. Also, the courts have adopted many criteria of bigness. Economists differ widely in their definitions of bigness and in their estimate of its being good or evil.

The technical advantage of bigness is attacked on the

ground that there is an optimum size of the unit of production which is far below the combination of units comprising the inclusive corporation. Hence, it is argued, competition between the units is restricted. The divisions of
many corporations are frequently self-contained—then
why should they be united? Is not this superunity an evil?

On the other hand, it is pointed out that there are advantages of bigness other than economy in manufacturing.
Financing is easier and less expensive to obtain. Diversity
of products scatters risk. Trouble in any part of the organization can be attacked by the keenest intellects, which
are likely to be more numerous and of higher quality than
in small organizations. Research on a large scale and over
a prolonged period can be done only by a big organization. The marketing system can be more accurately developed to fit the needs of the products and customers. The
marketing system may be adaptable to all the varied products which are manufactured, thus saving expense. Resources can be owned and controlled for smooth operation
in vertical integration. Big concerns are free to decide
whether to buy or make their parts, a choice which is
denied to smaller concerns. New products can be more
economically developed with the aid of existing facilities.

Perhaps most important of all, bigness concentrates on
assuring good management of all subordinate divisions.
The key positions of a large organization are sufficiently
attractive to obtain men of outstanding ability, and these
in turn demand high standards from their subordinates. It
is their sole function to see that each division is operated
with a maximum of skill. They ponder problems of amal-
gamating initiative with system, independence with control.

In contrast, the smaller concern attracts outstanding

ability spasmodically, so that after several generations it is likely to be caught in the doldrums or to embark on an unsuccessful new policy. The time span of management and that of a generation do not coincide. Normally, management is limited to fifteen or twenty years—i.e., some part of the age span between forty and sixty-five. Generations generally are in terms of twenty-five to thirty-five years. This creates in a concern, where the owner is the manager, an interim period between father and son, during which father has passed his prime and son has not arrived at maturity. This is not a definite law, but it is likely to occur.

The scales of management are weighted in favor of bigness. Nowhere is bigness more important than in innovation and risk taking. In the past, new ventures were entered into by groups of individuals backing a new idea or invention. That is how Henry Ford started. Steinway Pianos displays pictures of the little shop of the founder on Walker Street more than a hundred years ago. Woolworth, Kress, Kresge, and Lipton's Tea Company all grew out of a single tiny store. It was considered the normal process of free enterprise. The "idea" grew into a success and became incorporated. Nostalgic eyes look back upon those golden days. It was typical of the growth of today's giants. Such growth exists today, but it is not symbolic. Indeed, it is very rare if not impossible. Growth typically comes from the reaching out of one established corporation into new adjacent fields—either vertically or horizontally.

All of these trade advantages cannot be garnered by any one corporation. Some indeed are complementary, but many are in opposition. Bigness, organization, and trade custom supplement one another. An advantageous location is often more attainable by the smaller concern. Specialization is opposed to bigness. Reputation for excellence has its severe limits when applied to a variety of products. What is convenient for one group may be inconvenient for another. Exclusiveness and wide distribution are mutually opposed. Highest standards of quality are expensive to maintain, and cannot compete in price with utility.

For these reasons, trade position seldom develops into monopoly. Yet it is the ruling force of the economy. Without it, the daily operation must rely on sharp wits as in trading. Without it, each tomorrow must be faced anew. This is too precarious for the operation of continuous mass production. How trade position, innovation, and enterprise intertwine to create a dynamic economy will be explored further in later chapters.

5

THE TRADE POSITION OF
PATENTS

THE TRADE POSITION built up on the basis of the patent is
in important respects a variant of the types of industrial
trade positions discussed in the previous chapter. It seems
to warrant a separate analysis, for it depends on a monopoly granted by the government for a limited period
of seventeen years. This analysis concentrates on the extent of the trade position that can be won through ownership of a patented method or article. A patent does not
give the right to manufacture the article created by the
inventor, for this right exists without a patent. Rather, it
is the right to exclude others from manufacturing the
article without permission from the patentee. In a sense,
a patent is similar to any piece of private property which
may be used only by its owner or by permission of its
owner. But this advantage may be extended by conditions
of sale and stipulations in licensing. These conditions have
required the use by the licensee of articles not covered by
the patent; the kind or type of article permitted to be
manufactured, as well as the quantity; the territory in
which the licensee was permitted to sell; and the price—
either minimum or fixed—which he was required to
charge.

It is important to note that the license, as such, did not

create the monopoly. That was done by the grant of the patent. What the license did was to fix the terms on which the patentee surrendered his right to exclude the licensee from use of the patent. In this way a high degree of control has been sought and gained, sometimes over a large portion of an industry. These conditions of sale and licensing have in many cases been stricken down by Supreme Court decisions, which have even gone so far as to limit or nullify the monopoly granted by the patent.

The economic purpose of the patent law is to make technological progress promptly available to the public. The method is to stimulate invention and innovation through an opportunity of earning a generous reward. In attempting to carry out this purpose, American patent law has been patterned on that of England.

Patents date back to the reign of the first Queen Elizabeth. At this time, the objective was to increase manufacturing in England, and hence patents were granted for a period of fourteen years for any new article, whether an invention or an importation. During the sixteenth century patents were also granted as favors, causing much discontent. This led to the Statute of Monopolies (1624) in the reign of James I. This statute declared all monopolies void, but made an exception of granting a patent to the "true and first inventor" of any article. The patent monopoly thus became firmly entrenched in English law despite the growth of free enterprise.

Following this lead, early American law adopted the formula of "new and useful" as the test for issuing a patent. The anomaly of sanctioning a monopoly in an economy based on competition always made it difficult to fit the two concepts together and led to reluctant and partial acceptance of the benefits of granting patents. In the early years of the republic the need for encouraging manufacture overcame all theoretical objections. Inventions were few and infrequent, and of undoubted public benefit.

The law was broadened in 1836 and again in 1861 to stimulate "newness" and the "flash of genius." The period for which the patent ran was increased from fourteen to seventeen years. Emphasis was placed on protecting the skilled artisan, who required time for his training in the new method; the discovery of other and even better methods and articles; alternative ways of accomplishing improvement. The innovator was free to use, vend, or license his patent. There emerged the doctrine of diversification, i.e., that social needs were best served if there were many patents competing for and covering a choice of meeting the same needs. In theory, none was harmed by the innovation of a patent, for the former technique had served in the past and was still open.

Conditions changed the economic significance of the patent. The lone inventor working in the barn on his bright idea became less typical. In his stead laboratories grew up, expensively equipped and paid for from surplus earnings of large corporations. Since expense could be deducted from income, an increasing slice of expenses could be passed on to the government through decreased income taxes. In effect this subsidized research and innovation.

Work in the laboratory is aimed at correcting the specific weaknesses that show up when an article is in practical use. When rayon was first developed it was highly inflammable. Women were burned to death by the flick of a cigarette ash. Babies tucked in plucked rayon coverlets went up in flames. The future of the industry seemed dark indeed until the chemists found the formula that made rayon noninflammable. The oil industry introduced into lubricating oil chemicals that eliminated the formation of carbon in the cylinders. Plastics are now moulded into hundreds of articles including cups, rugs, soles for shoes, curtains, chairs, hardware, and automobile bodies. Airplane engines require increased heat resistance in their metals.

Invention became a business function with specific purposes. It ceased to be a thing apart, associated with a crank or wizard, but became integrated into the daily work. It intertwined with the established production system. The economics of the patent system adapted itself to these new conditions.

As inventions multiplied and as production methods were more interlocked, the patents ceased to be important as monopoly but became all-important bargaining devices for trade position—sometimes very powerful. These innovations were also linked by minor, improving changes. They became weapons as one company jealously guarded its rights and accused others of infringement. The new ideas were in some cases more than the embodiment of superior methods; they were essential to the art of improved and continuous production. A manufacturer ultimately might not survive without the benefit of a new method developed by a rival.

Sometimes alternative methods were used by different companies. Finally one or the other proved to be better. Various devices came into practice to meet this situation. Research pooling by several corporations with full licensing reduced the expense of research and at the same time protected each participant from being confronted by the superior method of a competitor. Multicompany agreements exchanged patents on the basis of a stipulated royalty. At times, these limited the field or method of use of the new article.

The skillful manipulation of the patent right opened up the possibility of joining this advantage to other acquired trade advantages so as to enhance greatly the strength and permanence of a trade position. Several patents could be combined so as to accomplish a degree of control far beyond that which might result from the sum of the individual patents. Or they could be so interwoven with unpatented materials or products as to extend greatly their field of control. In thus extending control beyond the patent grant, the practices of licensing collided with the Sherman Act. A long succession of court decisions defined the tenuous line between them.

The Hartford-Empire case is an extreme and exceptional illustration of the expansion of trade position based on patents. This has been the subject of so many articles in legal journals that a detailed description appears unwarranted. The salient point, however, is appropriate. With the change of the glass industry from hand-blown to mechanically made products, the patents for the various processes came into the possession of a few companies, among which Hartford Fairmont (mainly owned by a group of businessmen not associated with the industry) and Empire Machine Company (a subsidiary of the Corning Glass Works) were dominant. These two established a system of cross-licensing and also licensed their machines to others. In order to simplify the complex structure which was thus created, they joined together as Hartford Empire, a corporate institution to which they ceded all their patents. Hartford Empire thus controlled over 700 necessary patents, and leased the glass-making machines on terms which controlled the type of glass permitted to be made. The machinery to manufacture so-called oven glass was restricted to Corning. Its trade name, Pyrex, became synonymous with oven glass in common usage. This led to confusion after competition set in.

With this pressure, they were able to force other important glass manufacturers into the combine: Hazel-Atlas, makers of glass containers; Thatcher, maker of milk bottles; Ball Brothers, makers of fruit jars; and Lynch Manufacturing Company, principal competitor of Hartford Empire in the manufacture of machinery.

By a series of agreements and the purchase of other patents, Hartford Empire eventually gained control of the supplementary machinery, such as formers, stackers, and lehrs, which in addition to feeders were necessary for the automatic manufacture of glassware. Hartford Empire thus achieved a dominant status in the control of the glass industry. This control was further bolstered by the activities of the Glass Container Association of America, which through a statistical committee discouraged licensees from increasing production and newcomers from entering the field. The profits from the patent leases were divided among the participants. In general, the leases were designed to permit outsiders to live.

Thus the trade advantage given by individual patents was extended to well-nigh complete control. Mr. Justice Roberts in his decision described it as follows:

In summary, the situation brought about in the glass industry, and existing in 1938, was this: Hartford, with the technical and financial aid of others in the conspiracy, had acquired, by issue to it or assignment from the owners, more than 600 patents. These, with over 100 Corning controlled patents, over 60 Owens patents, over 70 Hazel patents, and some 12 Lynch patents, had been, by cross-licensing agreements, merged into a pool which effactually controlled the industry. This control was exercised to allot production in Corning's field to Corning, and that in restricted classes within the general container field to Owens, Hazel, Thatcher, Ball, and such other smaller manufacturers as the group agreed should be licensed. The result was that 94% of the glass containers manufactured in this country on feeders and formers were made on machinery licensed under the pooled patents. (323 U.S. 386 [1938])

The patent also plays an important role (with variations) in many other industries, notably plastics, oil, chemicals, rubber, and drugs. In the course of limiting patent rights strictly to the patent itself, and of not permitting any enlargement of these rights to nonpatented articles or the restrictions regarding price, the courts have gone even further. They have denied the rights to exclude others, by requiring that the patentee grant a license on fair terms.

Compulsory licensing of a patent has long been a subject of debate. In 1912, and again in 1914, the Oldfield bills were before Congress. In 1922 came the Stanley Bill, and in 1940 the McFarlane Bill. All were rejected, mainly on the ground that they favored the large company as against the small one. It was pointed out that many small companies were dependent on the exclusive rights granted by the patent, and were unable to protect themselves by other means available to large companies.

In a 1926 decision of the Supreme Court regarding price provisions in licensing by the General Electric Company, it was held that the conditions were "normally and reasonably adopted" and required no further control. (272 U.S. 476)

This position has been reversed in recent years through a series of court and consent decrees. Stripped of legal verbiage, the issue is presented as to whether the conditions of the license go beyond the article or method patented and seek to control the sale of unpatented articles or to fix the price at which the article is sold. When this is the case, the license is null and void.

An interesting and complex example is the case of the Gypsum industry. United States Gypsum Company (USG) licensed four companies under its patents, with provisions controlling prices and methods of distribution, process, and machinery. The lower courts, following the General Electric precedent, upheld these provisions on the ground that the separate licenses were legal. But the Supreme Court, on appeal, reversed this decision, holding that the mutual knowledge of both the licensor and licensees constituted an unlawful conspiracy and monopoly. The Court declared that "Regardless of motive, the Sherman Act barred patent exploitation of the kind that was here attempted." License agreements which controlled practically an entire industry, and which were entered into with knowledge on the part of the licensor and licensees of the adherence of others, with control over prices and methods of distributions through agreements and through bulletins issued by the licensor, were held to be sufficient to establish a prima facie case of conspiracy in violation of the Sherman Act. Moreover, royalties were paid to USG on the basis of all gypsum board manufactured, whether patented or not. This decision precipitated a series of suits and appeals, several times going up to the Supreme Court and back to lower courts, that covered a period of five years, 1949–54.

The consent decree is the usual method of adjusting trade relations. These decrees have come to conform to a common pattern, of which the case of United States Rubber Company is typical. First, the decree states that it is arrived at "without trial or adjudication of any issue of fact or law." Next it terminates all existing agreements, amendments, and understandings, and goes into detail covering the practices to be enjoined in the future. The licensing provisions of patents are reviewed, so that restricting clauses are removed. This leads naturally to the opening up of a provision such as would include nonexclusive licenses granted to any applicant on equal terms.

The consent decree of Servel is similar in its provisions. Servel was ordered to grant to any applicant a "nonexclusive license to make, use, or vend absorption refrigeration units" under patents which they now owned or which they might acquire during the next five years. Such license must grant a full and unrestricted power to sublicense. However, "a reasonable nondiscriminatory royalty may be charged." If the parties cannot agree to a reasonable royalty, upon application, the court will fix the amount. Moreover, Servel must furnish technical assistance and information to the licensee at cost.

Clearly, the opposite extreme points of view; first, that patents are not subject to antitrust; and second, that all restrictions placed by the patentee in licensing are beyond the orbit of the patents and hence are subject to antitrust, have been rejected. What seems to be the prevalent point of view is that patents, like other private property, are subject to antitrust action when they overstep the limits of the patent granted and create a conspiracy or monopoly beyond the rights granted to them. The question in each case resolves itself into whether control falls within the rights of the patentee, or whether it extends beyond the limits of those rights.

The case of multiple cross-licensing is a controversial issue. The general case (if there be such) is one in which several companies hold patents on different processes, each necessary to the manufacture of the finished product. The cracking process of oil is an example. Each company is estopped unless it can gain the right to use the patents of others. There are differences of opinion as to whether the right to multiple licenses may be confined to the companies holding one of the essential patents, or whether this right must be extended to others. The proper method of fixing royalties is also in dispute. One school asserts that each royalty should be arrived at separately. Others claim that this is often not practical, and that a more generalized method is necessary.

The present status of the patent reflects the complex nature of industry. Individual inventions and innovations still go on, though they play a decreasingly important role. The big contribution comes from the laboratories of the corporations. It was estimated by the Bureau of Labor Statistics (in January, 1953) that one fourth of all engineers and scientists are engaged in research. Compulsory licensing, though rejected by Congress on several occasions, has come to pass through the instrument of consent decrees. Great extensions of power are hampered by court orders to license patents at a fair royalty. The definition of "fair" constitutes a problem. It seems to resolve itself into an arm's-length agreement between the parties involved.

Lacking such agreement, the court may step in, and settle the matter. In practice, this seems to work, despite confusion; for there are normally many other methods of gaining trade position open to companies having large research departments. But naturally there is complaint that the patent law has been nullified, and there is dissatisfaction over specific cases.

Necessarily, this attempt to analyze the patent situation is so compressed that it can take up only those aspects related most closely to trade position. The court decisions and the literature are voluminous. For the patent law has always been, and still is, in flux, constantly being modified or extended. This confusion might seem to weaken the stimulus to invention. Yet, so great is the momentum of research, both in industry and government, and the need for it so urgent, merely to prevent dropping behind the procession, that new articles, new devices, and new methods continue to pour forth in an unbroken flow.

6

THE TRADE POSITION OF
FINANCIAL INSTITUTIONS

FINANCIAL INSTITUTIONS comprise all types of organizations dealing in money and credit, including national banks, state banks, private banks, investment houses, credit instruments of the federal government, specialized credit corporations, insurance companies, and loan associations.

Of these, banks, both public and private, are most deeply concerned with their trade position. Hence this chapter concentrates on banks and relegates to a minor place the other types of financial institutions. Moreover, it is limited to an analysis of trade position of banks, rather than treating banking as a whole. It is concerned with recounting the combination of circumstances which gave to the banks a powerful trade position prior to 1913, and of the subsequent progressive deterioration of those circumstances.

Banks were perhaps the earliest institutions to achieve a trade position. This advantageous position was directly due not only to the use of their own capital, but also to the control of the large sums for which they were the repositories. Within the limits of "sound" banking principles, this amount was at their disposal for investment.

In carrying out its obligation to adopt a sound monetary policy, Congress created the first Bank of the United

States in 1791 and the second in 1816, each with considerable freedom of policy. An advantageous trade position was thus conferred on these banks by government. These banks had the further obligation of facilitating the finances of the federal government. Suspicion accumulated that this advantage was being abused by political activities and for personal aggrandizement, so that the charter of the second Bank was not renewed in 1837. This period was then followed by wildcat competitive state and local banking, with all the disorder and chaos that must necessarily result from such a situation. This confusion was considerably, though not wholly, alleviated by the passage of the National Bank Act in 1863. State bank notes were replaced by the more uniform national bank notes. Banks were brought under progressively improved supervision. The growing importance of private banks, however, counteracted these improvements, for they were unregulated and controlled large deposits. Moreover, private bankers came to wield great influence over the policies of the national banks.

Inquiry into the principles of "soundness" in banking prior to the establishment of the Federal Reserve System leads to varied opinions, depending on the location of each bank. Since each bank had to rely largely on itself, it carried a considerable amount of cash in its own vaults. The minimum of soundness was apparently about 10 percent of deposits, but a more usual estimate of conservativeness was 20 percent. Loans deposits or investments readily convertible into cash brought the total of liquid assets up to 50 percent of deposits. Anything less was speculative or "unsound."

Materially higher ratios were common. The remaining

50 percent might be invested in sound but longer term mortgages, bonds, and loans, including slow loans. Holding of stock should be limited to paid-in capital. The generally accepted ratio of capital to deposits was 1 to 4 or 5.

There were many departures from this rough formula, due to both local conditions and personalities. Country banks kept deposits with city banks, counting them as immediately available. City banks deposited their reserves with New York city banks. New York banks carried a long line of call loans on stock exchange collateral. The exact position of private bankers was known only to themselves, and probably fluctuated widely.

Central holding of reserves thus came into being, without public design or control. The New York banks, holding the pyramided reserves of the country, used them to enhance their own power and profit. The result was to stiffen financial crises. Deposits could readily be withdrawn when there was no special need for them, but when the country banks needed their reserves because of industrial depression, call loans had to be liquidated on a falling stock market. Thus crises intensified and led at times to a complete lack of liquidity and suspension of specie payments. Through the deft manipulations of the deposits at their disposal, banks were able to dominate the financial affairs of many railroad and industrial companies, thus bringing to themselves further deposits and further influence.

This situation gave the bankers, both national and private, a strong voice in determining the present and the future of commercial, industrial, and railroad ventures. There was a constant temptation to stretch the rules of sound banking. Success generated further deposits which in time increased the influence of the New York banks. Losses caused by default on loans which could not be met out of capital or reserves were shared by depositors. Meanwhile, in the 1880s, the country was developing apace. Investments were being poured into first railroads and later manufacturing. Such investments necessarily had a speculative tinge (using the word "speculative" in its proper and not derogatory sense) so that when they went bad, banks suffered. It has been aptly said that the development of the country during this period was based on the insolvency of banks.

The National Monetary Commission under the guidance of Senator Aldrich in 1908 brought to light the dangers of an inelastic currency, the faulty structure of the banking system, and the perilous manner of handling reserves. The Pujo Committee report in 1913 revealed the intermeshing of interests and personalities that underlay the dominant position of the banking group. Especially influential was the group dominated by J. P. Morgan & Company. Through their influence over the First National Bank, the National City Bank, and the Guaranty Trust Company, they exercised a degree of control over industry which was commonly referred to as a "money trust" or monopoly. It was neither of these, but it was very strong. Other private bankers referred to them as the "Corner," owing to their location on Wall and Broad Streets in New York, and customarily asked their approval before undertaking any important new policy or development. Independent, though cooperative, were private banking houses, especially Kuhn Loeb & Company, Lee Higginson

& Company, Kidder Peabody, the Chicago banks and the growing California banks. Each of these established a strong position in certain industries.

The banking position of vantage rested on an intermeshing of the use of the bank's available resources, the marketing of corporate securities from time to time, and influence over the borrowing corporation's finances and policies through a place on the board of directors. This usually resulted in the bank's holding the deposits of the corporation as well as taking charge of its financial transactions. It also included advance information of business transactions of the corporations.

As a result, the act creating the Federal Reserve System was passed in 1913. The System was given important powers to provide an elastic currency and to improve the supervision of banks; and these powers became part of a broad objective of regulating the flow of credit and money in order to permit stable economic growth. It scarcely touched the combination of circumstances which gave a dominant position to the important private bankers.

With the end of World War I this combination of circumstances began to alter. Financial operations became scattered. New firms gained in importance and achieved a modicum of independence. The decade of the twenties saw the rise of industrial leaders strong enough to challenge the financiers. The stock market collapse of 1929 and the depression of the thirties completed the destruction of financial control. The shaky position in which many banks found themselves necessitated defense efforts, and left little play for maintaining influence. Cooperation suffered when each was intent on his own troubles. Public outcry forced new legislation which strengthened government influence over the Federal Reserve System. Registration of security issues and margin requirements in carrying securities were initiated. Deposit accounts were insured up to $5,000 and later up to $10,000. Perhaps the coup de grâce was delivered in the divorcement of commercial banking operations from underwriting of security issues.

At this time, other institutions of finance increased in importance, especially insurance companies, savings banks, and personal loan companies. Total investments of life insurance companies have risen from $7½ billion in 1920 to $73 billion in 1952 and $84 billion in 1954. The public scramble for security has led to great concentration of investment funds. The largest life insurance company has assets of over $8 billion, the ten largest together have $50 billion.

Following the New York state investigation of 1905, insurance policies and investments had become closely regulated by state laws. Legal investments must conform to strict requirements. Within these limits, however, there remains a considerable degree of freedom of choice. So great is their lending power, that one or a group of insurance companies may buy the entire new issue of a corporation running into tens of millions, and on a few occasions into the hundreds of millions.

Moreover, their investment choice has been extended to the direct ownership of real estate and securities of selected corporations. This has given to some of the big companies unique power in slum clearance and redevelopment of great portions of many cities. Such developments, fostered by the right of eminent domain exercised by municipalities, have widespread effect on adjacent real estate, transport systems, power companies, and many individual enterprises. Investment in common stocks by insurance companies is probably so hedged in that it has little contributory effect.

Specialized needs for credit by both business and consumers, which banks normally were unable to supply, led to the creation of specialized credit institutions. The growth of personal finance companies, while not so great as that of the insurance companies, has been spectacular. In 1920 their importance was negligible. In 1929, their total installment credit was $2.7 billion, only to drop off to $1½ billion during the depression. It rose to over $5 billion in 1940–41, to fall again to $2 billion during World War II when it was reduced by regulation. A period of rapid growth started in 1946. By 1953, the total of such loans had reached $20 billion, and the growth has continued.

Government credit institutions have also risen to importance. The Reconstruction Finance Corporation, the Commodity Credit Corporation, and the Federal Housing Administration are the most conspicuous among a vast system of bureaus granting specialized credits or guarantees.

Since World War II new forms of concentrated capital have come into being. Pension funds, investment companies, and personal trusts managed by banks and business counselors have increased rapidly. As estimated by Mr. G. Keith Funston, president of the New York Stock Exchange, institutional holdings of common and preferred stocks have jumped from about $11 billion in 1945 to about $32 billion in 1955. Personal trusts administered by banks are estimated at about $37 billion. Moreover, they are growing at an increasing rate. In 1945 their rate of growth was $250 million per year, against a recent rate of $1½ billion per year.

A new concentration of financial power seems in the making. The net result of this growth of new financial institutions is that the great, advantageous trade position of commercial banks at the turn of the century has been whittled away to a mere shadow. The commercial banker has lost position through the decreased importance of commercial loans in an economy of continuous production and distribution. He has developed compensatory services—transfer agent for securities, safekeeping of securities, trusteeship, investment advice.

But these constitute a sorry substitute for his loss.

7

THE TRADE POSITION OF
LABOR UNIONS

THERE SEEMS NO DOUBT that labor unions first grew as a "countervailing power" (to adopt the apt phrase coined by Professor J. K. Galbraith) designed to establish some degree of equality of bargaining strength between the employer and the individual employee. Bitterly opposed by both employers and government in the nineteenth century, labor unions slowly gained recognition through a series of crises—a story that needs no repetition here. Slowly the opinion spread (though questioned by a minority) that the competitive bargaining procedure of the market place, when confined to individuals, brought results which were compatible neither with social justice nor with the national welfare.

Few of the assumptions underlying the operation of a free market existed in 1890. The individual worker frequently had a minimum mobility. He had limited monetary resources or suffered from lack of knowledge of other opportunities; sometimes he was driven closely by necessity. Normally a surplus of labor was available. On the other hand, employers were so few in number that their actions affected the market; they normally had superior financial resources; they had the ability to import laborers from other sections of the country or from Europe. An extramarket mechanism was clearly called for to correct the inequality of bargaining power. This was supplied by the organization of the labor union.

Organization of powerful labor unions was sporadic until the 1930s. They were first generally recognized as an important part of the structure of industry during World War I, in which the American Federation of Labor representatives played a considerable part on many committees of government. Their increased membership, arriving at a peak of about five million, enhanced their influence. But during the twenties their membership shrank to about two million. Their influence receded accordingly.

Government help during the Roosevelt administration, the passage of the Wagner Act and the Norris–LaGuardia Act barring injunctions, helped them to achieve a new and greatly enhanced position in the economy. Capable leaders took over the task of organizing, and they increased membership from 3.6 million in 1935 to 8 million in 1940. By 1945, during the war years, the total membership had increased to 12.6 million, and by 1954 it was estimated at over 17 million. This 17 million is to be related to the estimated 45 million (more or less) comprising the organizable labor force.

The union owes its trade position to the strategic use of the strike, reenforced by skillful organization. Through this weapon it is able to inflict on the employer damage calculated to bring him into a more receptive state of mind at the settlement table. If the strike alone does not bring about a satisfactory bargain, it can be reenforced by the picket line, the secondary strike, and the boycott. The history of labor shows that threats and violence have not been absent—on either side.

The strike is an inherited institution, the character of which has greatly changed. In the 1880s and 1890s it sometimes approximated open warfare, with government on the side of law and order. Hence, public officials opposed destructiveness on the part of strikers. The conflict centered on the ability of the strikers to hold out and of the company to avoid destruction. Generally the company won. Because the strike was typically local, the public interest was but slightly affected. Gradually strikes grew in size. As they came to include an entire industry, either in a locality or wider territorial division, all industry and a large segment of the public were harassed and injured. The stoppage of any section of the economy, no matter how small, causes repercussions that affect disinterested parties.

The "general strike" loomed on the horizon. The public interest became involved. Therewith the rules of the game were tightened until the strike took on the aspects of a medieval tournament, or, better still, a boxing match under Marquis of Queensbury rules with alert referees. Yet the strike can be a fearful instrument, especially when the rules are violated.

With the so-called collective bargaining between labor and management, it was hoped that reasonable agreements on terms of employment and wages might result in greater justice than at the market place. The appeal to "natural" forces becomes remote, especially in the case of industrywide agreements. The only natural force involved is in interindustry competition, in which influence is tempered by many obstacles. Within these limits the competitive ability of labor leaders to bring improved conditions to their members is a more powerful stimulant.

Indeed, the moderate labor leader whose judgment is swayed by ultimate developments rather than immediate results finds himself at a disadvantage with the less well-informed membership of his union. Comparative wage increases in one union or another are paraded against him. Many forces converge in opposition to the wisdom of labor contracts. In the Gompers era of a comparative lack of bargaining strength, the policy of the union could be well be "more and always more." Such a policy is incompatible with the growth of strength. In the long run it can defeat itself, and contracts involve the long run. A continuation of the methods applicable to the winning of a strong trade position becomes exploitation after the strong position has been attained. Exploitation leads to loss of a trade position.

Such a result seems already evident in the coal industry. The cost of the delivery of natural gas is markedly less than that of coal to many communities, so that the decline in the use of coal has probably been hastened. The ports of New York and San Francisco have both suffered through the general losses caused by waterfront strikes which have severely affected many interests beyond the parties involved. Imperceptibly, labor unions have emerged from a countervailing force into one of original strength.

The key position in bringing general pressure is held by the transportation industry. The railroad unions were the first to exploit this advantage; they have been followed by trucking and shipping unions. But a strong position can be gained in any industry when it is taken as a whole. The industry-wide bargaining conference adds a new note of advantage to the trade positions of unions.

The strike of a few tugboat workers in New York harbor

caused the destruction of quantities of fresh food and the suffering of large numbers of the population. The impact of a strike of milk deliverymen falls mainly on babies, children, mothers, and patients in hospitals. The steel strike of 1952 closed up many industries including the automobile industry, put many people out of work, and affected profits to such an extent as to throw the tax calculation of the government into disorder. The losses due to the strike in the canning industry fell upon the Florida citrus fruit industry, whose crop was just ripening.

The strike shifted from a trial of strength between employers and employees to a process of victimizing outsiders and the public in general. The necessity for settlement of a strike comes not from union or management but from external sources having nothing to do with the issues involved. The milk strike and the steel strike ended with an increase in wages and a rise in the price of milk and steel, results which satisfied both labor and management. The public bore the loss of the strike and again the cost of settlement.

A labor-management joint conference is always ill adapted to substitute reason for the market place. Whereas the individual employees were helpless in their bargaining with management the union was adapted to equalize their relative bargaining strengths. Developments have gone far beyond this original purpose.

In the process of gaining a strong position, unions achieved several immunities:

1. The right of members to hold their present jobs while on strike, including security and other perquisites.

2. Exemption from antitrust statutes, including conspiracy.
3. Industrywide wage rates and conditions.
4. Acquiescence in occupying company property.
5. The ability to slow down production.
6. The closed shop or the union shop.
7. The enforced collection of dues.
8. The arbitrary discipline over members.
9. The arbitrary exclusion of applicants.
10. A degree of control over pensions.

Not all of these rights and immunities prevail in every case, nor are they all necessary. Taken together, they elevate the employee from individual helplessness to joint dominance. Willing managements might have rendered the winning of many of these rights unnecessary; unwilling managements had them forced down their throats. The resistance of management continues, but it is at low ebb.

The trade position of labor unions is one of unstable equilibrium. Criticism of their policies is increasing. Unions have lost that sympathy naturally inherent with the weaker party. The public is associating demands for higher wages with higher prices, which everyone must pay. The fact that labor has no control over price, though it can force wages up, constitutes a critical weakness in its trade position. When a strike forces prices up, labor loses public support necessary to maintain the legal safeguard of collective bargaining.

Unions are being blamed by some for the shipping decrease in the ports of San Francisco and New York. One estimate blames John L. Lewis for the decline in the use of coal. The *Wall Street Journal* has put it aptly:

Economically, Mr. Lewis wrung from the operators all that the business would bear. His strikes, and threats of strikes, and his success, had effects other than higher wages and welfare royalties. They had also the effect of raising the price of hard coal, and the effect of turning users of hard coal to other methods of heating.

Technologically, Mr. Lewis probably did more to promote the gas and oil industries than he foresaw or intended to do. Lines were laid to pipe natural gas into the New England area from the Southwest. Aside from the price, and the fear that future strikes might cut off their supply of coal, people found gas and oil cleaner and less troublesome.

With the achievement of labor's strong trade position, new countervailing forces are emerging. The collective bargaining procedure has become institutionalized. In many industries it has evolved into a joint discussion to arrive at a mutually satisfactory arrangement. In some industries strikes are unknown. Unions help employers to increase productivity in order that they may meet competition. The International Ladies' Garment Workers Union is a pioneer in this policy. Unions have instituted a system of shop stewards, who smooth out many tangles before they become important. Typically, they adopt a wise and judicious attitude in settling individual real or fancied grievances. In many cases a high level of mutual understanding between shop stewards and the personnel administration of management has replaced antagonism. The working agreements hammered out locally far outnumber the irreconcilable differences that lead to the calling of a strike. But they are not so well publicized. The days lost in strikes have shrunk as low as one fourth or one fifth of one percent in some years. The attitudes and policies of unions in different industries, as well as the attitudes of management, vary widely.

Many companies have a profit-sharing plan in operation. While these differ greatly in detail, they all have as their objective the identification of higher wages with the success of the company rather than with bargaining. Managements also are setting out to woo the loyalty of their employees. The Lincoln Electric Company of Cleveland is not unique in this respect. It has a system for paying bonus wages based on annual profits.

Mr. James F. Lincoln says in his book *Incentive Management:* "The results so far obtained by incentive management are very great compared to what is usual in industry with so-called collective bargaining." Through his philosophy of fostering cooperation between management and employees, his records claim to show that since 1934, the prices of the products of Lincoln Electric have had a downward tendency, whereas the prices of other companies in the same industry have had a tendency to rise. Average wages are higher than in any other company, and the margin of advantage has widened. In the earlier years, the margin averaged around 50 or 60 percent; in later years, it has hovered around 100 percent. The sales product per employee was more than double the average in the electric industry.

Since 1947 the General Electric Company has put into practice a revised policy in regard to collective bargaining. An effort is made to arrive at a fair result, agreed to by both sides, not by trading but by keeping in mind the other factors of production. General Electric places on the same level its relations to customers, stockholders, employees, suppliers, and the public, and strives to satisfy all equally. More recently, United States Steel and United Steelworkers of America have been emphasizing their mutual interests, rather than their antagonism.

Sears Roebuck is outstanding in its efforts to bind together the interest of the company and the employee. Through their ingenious stock purchase plan, every employee is given the opportunity of participating in profits gained by successful operation. This practice is becoming increasingly widespread.

Such methods, as well as pension funds, knit the interests of the employee and the corporation more closely together. The practical difficulties are great, especially in the case of large corporations; but they seem capable of solution.

It may be that cooperation between management and labor is developing into a countervailing force to challenge the methods of antagonistic collective bargaining.

Just as the trade position of finance appeared for a time to be impregnable but proved to be temporary, so the trade position of labor unions may be more vulnerable than appears to the outside observer. In a dynamic economy, new techniques and methods are constantly emerging to challenge the old.

8

THE TRADE POSITION OF
AGRICULTURE

THE METHOD OF PRICING IN AGRICULTURE conforms more
nearly to the classical postulates than does that of any
other field: there are many buyers and sellers, all powerless, a market place where traders meet; supply and demand dominate. Without government supports agricultural
prices vary widely in response to the balance of market
changes at any given moment of time. Yet for many staples,
such as wheat, corn, potatoes, or cotton, neither supply
nor demand is very elastic with reference to prices. In
the short run, variations of supply depend much more
on the weather or on technological improvements than
on the price. If demand increases and prices rise, supply
cannot respond quickly. If prices go down, owing to an
abnormally large yield, the time lag operates to maintain
or even increase production, thus increasing carry-over
stocks. Since the bulk of production is on individually
owned farms and wage labor is not ordinarily an important
factor, farmers are individually powerless to restrict production as do manufacturers. Yet falling prices do not
usually stimulate demand in any marked degree, as is
the case in many manufactured products. Consumer demand for food is relatively steady, no matter what the
price. A lower price is more likely to stimulate the demand

for better quality than for increased quantity. As a result, the market price system does not bring about the equilibrium which is beneficial either to production or the allocation of resources.

Farmers have lucky breaks as well as bad breaks. Reduction of yield in one area increases demand for the products of other areas. But the years of crop failures cause hardships that leave scars. The range of variation of production nationally or the world over is relatively small, but locally it is very wide.

The range of price variations in an uncontrolled produce market is wide. The average price index of food grains in 1937 was 120; in 1938, 75; in 1939, 72. Even in the comparatively prosperous years from 1922 to 1929, the range in the average seasonal price of corn was from a low of 65 cents per bushel to a high of 84 cents per bushel; in wheat the range was from 92 cents to $1.21; in oats from 37 cents to 47 cents; in barley from 50 cents to 74 cents; in potatoes from 53 cents to $1.70. In cotton the range was from 17 cents to 28 cents per pound. In lesser crops, such as soybeans, hay, fruit, and truck, the range was on a similar scale.

In 1932, the ratio of prices of commodities bought by farmers to the averages of 1910–14 had fallen by 32 percent; but the ratio of prices of products sold by farmers was down by 42 percent. When variation of price is added to the variation in the size of crops due to disease, drought, and floods, it is clear that prosperity depends on circumstances largely beyond the control of any individual farmer. In contrast, the costs of harvesting, grading, packaging, transportation, selling at both wholesale and retail, and spoilage remain relatively constant.

Rendered helpless by utter lack of control over prices and quantity produced, farm leaders have made a series of attempts to organize marketing cooperation. These attempts have been failures in the staple crops except in a few sporadic cases.

As agriculture gradually changed in character from the self-sufficient farm to the commerical farm, a process well under way by 1880, markets became increasingly important to the individual farmer. This was particularly true of the new Western farmers, who typically had larger acreage than either those in the South or in the Northeast. At this period the South was protected by the voracious demand for cotton—both domestic and foreign.

In 1867, largely through the persistence of Oliver H. Kedley, the National Order of the Patrons of Husbandry, later known as the Grange, was formed. In addition to their social and cultural objectives, Granges were organized to buy cooperatively. They even attempted to manufacture farm equipment and machinery. These ventures ended in failure, and the Granges' membership dropped from more than 800,000 in 1875 to just over 100,000 in 1880, at which figure it remained for two decades.

The National Farmers Alliance was a grouping of many state alliances, mainly in the Southwest, which began in the early seventies. It reached its peak in the late eighties when it organized politically as the People's party and nominated a presidential candidate who drew over a million votes.

By 1900 most of the farm movements had collapsed; only the Granges remained. This left room for the formation of the Farmers Educational and Cooperative Union which spread throughout the South. The Union sought to control prices by refusing to sell for less than specified amounts—through holding supplies off the market. But this proved impractical, and the effort disintegrated. The American Society of Equity at about the same time attempted a like method in the Northwest. Though it claimed membership of over a million at one time, it also ended in failure; some of its remnants merged with the Union.

The long and dismal record of this series of attempts to establish a trade position for agriculture comparable to that achieved by manufacturing and distributing companies finally made it clear that by themselves farmers could not succeed. But farmers had another source of strength—votes. Even though their percentage of the total population has continuously shrunk, it is still considerable. The concentration of farm population in certain areas gives them more than proportionate political power locally. An increasing number of industries are dependent on farm prosperity. Farm organizations turned to the government for help, and in the end were not disappointed.

By 1910 government was already playing an increasingly important role. The Department of Agriculture became more active in promoting education. State educational and experimental stations were organized and were spreading scientific knowledge. State farm bureaus under county agents became the focal point of farmers' interests. A national organization of farm bureaus was formed in 1920, and in 1921 it represented forty-two states under the title of the Farm Bureau Federation. It was to serve the business and economic interests of farmers, as well as their educational and production problems. But its major success lay in the political field. As demand slackened in the middle twenties, Presidents Coolidge and

Hoover attempted a variety of patched-up measures to raise prices. This was, however, a period of discussion and disagreement, typified by five unsuccessful versions of the McNary-Haugen plan. It resulted finally in the recognition of agriculture as a "special national interest requiring a special public policy."

Farmers' lobbies and the farm bloc have always been vociferous in looking after their interests. The Secretary of Agriculture came to assume a group responsibility which has no parallel in that of the Secretary of Commerce or the Secretary of Labor. He inclined to devote himself exclusively to his group generally with a minimum interest in the national economic viewpoint.

The sporadic state help, scattered farm bureaus and experimental stations, and statistical services, taken together, have tended to improve the returns to agriculture. Finally, in the 1930s, federal legislation inaugurated a system of rigid price supports for basic commodities, implemented by numerous methods including curtailed acreage, marketing agreements, and the accumulation of government owned stocks. One prominent instrument was the Commodity Credit Corporation. All these efforts up to the years 1938–39, however, did not accomplish more than to raise the average level of farm prices to 95 percent of the pre-World War I level. The tremendous upsurge of demand in the 1940s came to the rescue. Accumulated stocks were cleared, and shortages appeared.

The concept of parity is unique. It starts with the doctrine that a constant ratio between the prices which the farmer pays and the prices which he receives is nationally desirable because it maintains a constant demand for the products of industry. No one can dispute the general proposition that during a depression the products of industry have a relatively greater drop in quantity than in price as compared with the stability of quantity and fall in price of agricultural production. All statistical records confirm common observation. The "normal" ratio for parity was determined by the average of the years 1909 to 1914.

The formula for the measurement of parity has undergone amendments. In 1933 it was declared to be the policy of the Congress "to establish and maintain such balance between the production and consumption of agricultural commodities, and such marketing conditions therefor, as will reestablish prices to farmers at a level that will give agricultural commodities a purchasing power with respect to articles that farmers buy, equivalent to purchasing power of agricultural commodities in the base period." For all agricultural commodities except tobacco, the base period specified was August, 1909, to July, 1914. For tobacco it was designated as August, 1919, to July, 1929. This formula was continued with only minor changes until 1948. Parity was redefined so as to include incomes as well as prices. The definition of parity prices was substantially the same as that previously used, except that freight rates as well as taxes and interest payments were to be included in the formula. Parity of income was defined as "that per capita net income of individuals on farms from farming operations that bears to the per capita net income of individuals not on farms the same relation as prevailed during the period from August 1909 to July 1914."

The measurement of each commodity implied that the price of each should have advanced by the same percentage, and that the relationships between the prices of the various farm products should have remained the same.

But costs had not increased uniformly as among the various agricultural products. Tractors and other mechanical improvements had reduced greatly the man-hour requirements in growing wheat and many other field crops. Livestock production, and some types of crop operation, had not experienced similar reductions in real cost. Consequently, if both groups had equal percentage gains in price the result would be to make the production of wheat and other highly mechanized crops very profitable as compared to livestock and fruits and vegetables, where the need for increases was greatest.

The 1948 plan sought to overcome this difficulty by revising the base prices of the various commodities so that they would bear the same relationship to each other as in recent years. This was to be done by taking the average price for each commodity during the most recent ten-year period and multiplying it by the ratio of the general level of prices received by farmers for agricultural products in the base period, 1910 to 1914, to the general level of prices received by farmers in the most recent period. This would give the "adjusted base price." To obtain the new parity price this adjusted base price would be multiplied by the ratio of prices paid by farmers currently to the price paid by them in the 1910–14 period.

The maintenance of parity requires heroic action on the part of the Secretary of Agriculture. Compensation must be made for adjustment of the market place. One step leads to another. Loans to individuals have given way to loans against the product, with no individual liability. This is tantamount to actual purchase. When surpluses pile up, crops must be controlled, and the quickest method possible is reduction of acreage by an arbitrary percentage. Since production is a function of intensity of cultivation as well as of acreage, it does not change proportionately. The poorest acres are taken out of production. In spite of planning, a surplus of one year may become an increased surplus the following year, instead of the planned shortage, and this surplus may extend to the year following that. Many ingenious devices must be found to get rid of the surplus without too great losses and without market dislocation. Among those which have been tried are special food stamps for the unemployed, good only for the specified foods which are in surplus supply; allotting certain quantities at reduced prices for less important purposes; gifts to foreign countries in distress; school lunches; even outright destruction. Each of these has a limited merit, especially in an emergency. None is a permanent solution.

Meanwhile a vast regulatory organization has been created: county agents, inspectors, warehouse owners, marketers, economists. Since 1929 the number of employees in the Department has more than tripled. Some agencies concentrate on increasing production, others on decreasing production. Money awards are given for increasing the fertility of the soil and for conservation generally. Improved seeds and fertilizers are handed out or sold at cost. The price of milk is set for each shed by a board representing producers, distributors, and government.

There was a constant shift in commodities classified as basic—both additions and deletions. These basic crops included mainly wheat, cotton, corn, rice, tobacco, and peanuts, but at one time or another sugar beets, cane, rye, flax, barley, sorghum, and potatoes were included among them. In addition, under the so-called Steagall amendment, the Congress has brought under price support any crop for which the Secretary of Agriculture requested increased production.

The series of agricultural acts which have freed the farmer from the direct impact of the market place began with the creation of the Federal Farm Board in 1929. The $500,000 appropriated for the Board's use was insufficient. When this amount had been expended without perceptible results, the Board ceased to function; however, during the Roosevelt administration, by a series of acts from 1933 to 1936, the Agricultural Adjustment Administration replaced the Board without marked success. At long last the Commodity Credit Corporation, which had been formed in 1933, was given greater power by the act of 1938.

Each of these acts was a compromise between emergency need, an attempt at a permanent solution and political pressure. Each of these crises was heightened by the exceptionally wide shifts in demand during the depression of the 1930s and the war requirements of the 1940s. The oversupply of the 1930s was relieved by the short crops of 1934 and 1936. The war years of the 1940s were accompanied by a series of exceptionally large crops. Fortune came to the rescue of the Commodity Credit Corporation.

In the meantime the underlying philosophy of government aid was undergoing a change. This began with the motto "help the farmers to help themselves." It soon shifted to protecting the farmers from bankruptcy, which in turn merged into assurance of increased prosperity. This evolving philosophy was inextricably complicated by the emergencies caused by the varying conditions of the marketing of individual crops, each of which has its peculiarities, and political pressures. In effect, the Department of Agriculture becomes the marketing agency of the controlled basic crops, if not the principal risk bearer. In so far as the farmer is protected in the sale of his product by government, the result is increased and unstable prosperity for the farmer, purchased at great loss and expense by the government and taxpayers, and by the public through high prices. Of course, all this applies only to those crops designated as basic, the value of which is estimated at about 40 percent of the value of all crops. Hence the pressure to have more crops designated as basic. Other benefits, such as payment for soil conservation, improved roads, marketing information service, and irrigation, are scattered about in a more or less haphazard manner.

It has been said that price supports inevitably transfer the problems of marketing at least in part from the individual to the Department of Agriculture. The Department is ill equipped to cope with these problems, partly from its own lack of organization, partly from the rules imposed upon it, and partly because of the inherent difficulties involved. Mild and temporary dislocations can be eased over, but they become impossible when stocks get out of hand. Rigid supports encourage surpluses, for they induce the individual farmer to increase rather than decrease his production. Thus they encourage the misallocation of resources. Regulation of production appears only partially to offset this urge. The dilemma in which the Department finds itself can only be postponed with rigid price supports dictated by legislation. Only with flexibility can it be solved in a satisfactory manner.

Large unsold surpluses have a depressing effect on price,

through fear that the appropriations for support may not be renewed by the Congress. When food prices remain high, public approval of price supports wavers in spite of large production. Agricultural economists with great unanimity condemn the system of rigid price supports. Even the American Farm Bureau Federation and the National Grange oppose it. Yet price supports were inaugurated to ease the difficult situation of farmers arising from uncontrolled production, the exaggerated foreign demand of the war years, and wide price ranges. Unfortunately for the farmers, their trade position is not expressed in the normal course of commercial business as is the position of manufacturers and labor unions. It rests on appropriations by government, falling directly on taxpayers. Their advantageous position is therefore vulnerable to public resentment in a degree greater than that of the other groups.

The topic for debate is no longer whether government should intervene in supporting prices and regulating agricultural production. That point for the present is settled. The question now revolves around what kind of intervention should be used, how far it should go, the degree of flexibility of the support, and the extent of government responsibility for shortages, surpluses, and farm prosperity.

9

A SUMMARY OF
TRADE POSITION

FROM THE FOREGOING ANALYSIS it seems clear that the major problem of trade position centers in the industrial field.

The struggles of labor and agricultural organizations are directed toward attaining equality of position with industrial businesses (though this merges into an advantageous position of great strength). In contrast, a trade position in industry is a necessity in itself in order to maintain the flow of production and distribution. The trade position of the financial world was of a different nature. It lay in the influence of the investment of large funds belonging to others, and concentrated in one or a relatively few institutions. At its height it depended on the dominance of a few vibrant personalities. Government restrictions and the growth of the Federal Reserve System, combined with tactical errors by the bankers, broke down their almost predominant influence. The present concentration of investment resources in the great insurance companies is likewise so limited by regulations that it could scarcely achieve outstanding national importance. Their trade position rests on their ability to attract a continuous flow of funds rather than on their investment influence.

The necessity to achieve a trade position in industry leads to many developments. The achievement of a trade position in the distribution of any product gives to the management some degree of control over the continuous flow of distribution which must accompany mass production. As indicated above, control depends on many sources of trade advantage.

Total lack of trade position can only breed chaos as it has done in agriculture, the cut-rate drugstores, and the dress industry. The irregular and spasmodic demand of the market place, by itself, does not permit orderly production. This is particularly true in agriculture, for the foreign demand fluctuates widely.

In an industry of continuous production, when from time to time the demand falls off, stocks pile up at a disastrously rapid rate. If possible, a new source of demand must be developed—a new territory at home or abroad; a new economic level hitherto untouched; or a new, untapped use which had been served in some other way. There is no exact point at which it can be said that the trade position is sufficiently strong. Management must always have some new device in reserve which for the moment is inexpedient or unnecessary, but which can be pushed when the time is opportune.

The "just sufficient" strength may lead to a new strength capable of abuse; per contra, the dominant position may be whittled away. The high degree of concentration, or perhaps the increasing concentration of production into fewer hands, is noted and lamented by many observers. Chief among these are government officials and certain economists. Statistics have been multiplied to prove that a few companies in each industry, say three or four, produce 75 or 95 percent of the total products of the industry. By some this is considered evil, for each of the units has an interest in maintaining the stability of the industry and, in some ways, is capable of contributing to that stability in its rate of production, its trade customs, and its price structure. Each unit is aware that its actions are part of the structure in which the other units operate. Hence each has a double interest—that of maintaining its own stability, and that of maintaining the stability of the industry as a whole. From this fact it is concluded by some that the methods of the oligopolist are indistinguishable from the methods of the monopolist. Under this interpretation, the economy is described as *monopolistic capitalism,* essentially similar to true monopoly and cartelism.

The forces operating towards control are indeed very powerful; left to themselves they might well develop into a static monopoly. We must turn to the dynamic forces in the economy to discover why they seldom, if ever, work out to this logical conclusion.

Observation indicates that the most important dynamic factor is the research, both basic and applied, that is carried on throughout industry. As measured by the Department of Defense, this cost to industry is estimated to be about $1½ billion, and to government $2¼ billion. The total number of engineers and scientists engaged in research is placed at 180,000. The Bureau of Labor Statistics estimate is somewhat, though not much, lower. This research is not confined to physics and chemistry but extends to markets, habits of consumers, new raw materials and methods. Each concern must exploit this research as best it can, for it must hold its trade position. Each unit uses its research for innovation according to its best judgment. There is business loss as well as social gain in innovation. Innovations create obsolescence as well as cheaper or more efficient products. To withhold or postpone has its risks, for someone else may step in. Sears Roebuck has a policy of expansion, whereas Montgomery Ward has had a policy of sound contraction. It is charged that the American Woolen Company suffered because it was slow in adopting the latest developments in artificial fibers. As a result of constant innovations nothing remains as expected for a long period of time. New methods and products tend to multiply, for any important innovation induces adjustments and rearrangements of many related products and gadgets used in conjunction with it. The rate of innovation appears to be accelerating.

A new product may be developed from any of several sources. Synthetic rubber might stem from the rubber, chemical, or oil industry; detergents from the soap or the chemical industry; glass fibers from the chemical or glass industry. General Mills Company has a policy of expanding into any field that offers promise, regardless of its connection with former products. Most innovations (though not all) are a projection of the channel already existing, in some way related to, but at the same time strengthening the going organization.

It is not enough then, in adopting policy, for a unit to seek the welfare of its industry as well as of itself. Many industries are subject to forces from the outside, interweaving in a complex and subtle manner. As the price of leather goes down, the price of meat must go up if the total value of cattle on the hoof is to be maintained. Similarly, as the price of wool goes down, the difference must be made up by the price of lamb. It is said that 80 percent of the products sold by the Du Pont Company are new, in the sense that they have been developed in the last twenty-five years.

The constant procession of changes and improvements

throughout industry leaves only limited scope for complacency of management in its efforts to stabilize either its own position or that of the industry.

Measurements of monopoly and competition are tricky and elastic. Yet without measurement of some sort, one can hardly conclude judgments of "more or less." The standard often used by outside critics of industry (including government) has to do with structure of the industry. The point of view is that many units indicate much competition. If one unit drops out, or is absorbed, less competition is postulated. Freedom of entry into an industry indicates more competition. Impediments to free entry indicate less.

In contrast, the standard by which industrial management measures the absence of competition is the feeling of ability to carry out plans uninhibited by external nuisance forces. From this point of view any external innovation is a nuisance. All managements agree that innovation is constant and hence competition is keener than a generation ago. Managements are acutely conscious of the limits of their control, or the impingement of new forces to which they must adjust and readjust their policies and their operations.

The result is that the menace of concentration is viewed from different and incompatible points of view. The angle of the critics is static; that of management is dynamic. In a static economy the existence of few units leads more easily to cartel control arrangements than the existence of a thousand. But in a dynamic economy the boundaries of an industry are not so easily defined. Industries invade the territories of one another. Many products can be classified as belonging to several industries. New products arise as an extension of old products, deriving characteristics from any one of several sources. In a dynamic economy the threat of monopolistic control latent in oligopoly has only occasional and temporary opportunity to develop.

During the years 1946–50, when there was a shortage of automobiles, the "big three" manufacturers dared not raise their prices. The exploitation of the consumer that resulted from scarcity came from independent dealers and speculators. These are remnants of free enterprise, not products of present management. The big retail merchants have a policy of passing on to customers any lucky purchase or fortunate break in the market. The American Can Company and the Continental Can Company together manufacture over 80 percent of all cans. Yet each eagerly develops any new product or service that will enhance its share in the total. The "big four" companies vie with one another for a larger share of the total. Each cement company has a local advantage due to freight rates, yet each reaches into the territories of others to build up its volume.

A strong trade position should not be confused with monopoly. Monopoly signifies the power to fix prices at such point that the demand at those prices yields a revenue higher than could be achieved under competition. Even in this interpretation the power of monopoly is limited by the demand for the article monopolized. This depends on the necessity for the article, the classic example being salt. The unusual feature of monopoly is the lack of direct competition, which might further limit the control over price. Indeed, in perfect competition there is no control over the supply, the demand, or the price. The automatic forces of the market are in control.

A trade position is neither monopoly nor competition, though it bears a relation to both. It is a "more or less" ability to stabilize—not supply, but demand. The degree of this ability marks the strength and longevity of the trade position. As shown in the previous chapters, it rests on many sources, and each of these sources has limitations in strength and time.

Without any trade position, only supply and demand control prices. The natural fluctuation of these forces is so great that continuous mass production is impossible in a practical sense.

The actual problem, then, is not competition as opposed to monopoly, but the social and industrial benefit of various degrees or kinds of trade position. The structure of industry, finance, labor, or agriculture is too complex to permit any single simple criterion of value. Indeed, the lengthy, abstract decisions of the courts in interpreting the Sherman Act and its supplements indicate the necessity of coming to grips with social actuality rather than shadow-boxing behind inappropriate concepts and verbiage. Of necessity, the courts have had to build up their own value judgments, for these are either not supplied by legislation or are only vaguely indicated. Judicial value judgments are thus created by the considerations of the legal mind—not the concrete judgments of economists, philosophers, and practical men. At times these value judgments are sound from the economic viewpoint presented here, but more often they reflect the classical economic concepts.

From such a situation nothing but confusion could emanate. The Department of Justice and, to a lesser extent, the Federal Trade Commission concentrate on the

structure of industry. Administrators of corporations concentrate on the particular situation with which they are
confronted. Financiers operate within various boundaries
of convention, freedom of choice, and governmental control. Labor leaders have problems of organization. The
best hope of agricultural leaders is government assistance
through political pressure.

They have only one point in common: they all seek a
refuge from the vagaries of the market place. They all
attempt to modify or control the erratic confusion of automatic fluctuation; they all seek in the end to combine
steady flow of demand with expansion of demand—not
with the contraction which is thought to be the result of
monopoly.

10

COMPETITION AND
INNOVATION

IT IS NECESSARY TO INVESTIGATE why some economists be-
moan the decline of competition, whereas others feel that
competition is more active than ever before. All agree (at
least outwardly) that competition is the life of trade and
the basic reason for the success of the United States' economy. But the concept of competition seems to mean different things to different people.

To the traditional economist, the concept of competition is that laid out by Adam Smith and consistently followed for a century and a half. It still has many adherents.
It reaches the conclusion that if the assumptions which
underlie it do not fit the facts of the national economy,
then there is something wrong with the economy, which
should be changed. The development should be reversed
and made to conform with the ideal. When practices do
not fit the ideal, those practices are evil.

This ideal is an economy in which prices are determined
by an auction, or quasi-auction or bargain, participated
in by a large number of free agents, none of whom by himself is of sufficient importance to affect the price. This
is an economy in which price is the focal point, so that
what emerges is a *natural* price. Should any collusion or

interference through the use of power enter, then monopoly or conspiracy is thought to regulate the price. This cannot be tolerated. Monopoly is as bad as competition is good.

This was the concept of competition which underlay the thinking that produced the Sherman Act in 1890. It was based on an economy of units, each of which produced a single type of goods to be brought to market and sold singly. The illustrations concern mainly agricultural products, but it was supposed to apply to all industry. That it still dominates the thinking of the Federal Trade Commission (though increasingly questioned) is shown by recent complaints (in the Atlas case) and decisions of which the following quotation is a typical sample:[1]

Paragraph Seven: The effect of the discrimination in price knowingly induced, received, or accepted by the respondents and of the practices and activities hereinbefore found in connection with their purchases of "TBA" products, may be and is substantially to lessen competition in the lines of commerce in which the respondents are engaged and to injure, destroy, or prevent competition between respondents' suppliers of the aforesaid products who grant respondents lower prices on the one hand, and those suppliers who do not grant such discriminatory prices on the other, and also to injure, destroy, or prevent competition between respondents and other marketers, including distributors, wholesalers, jobbers, and others who do not receive the said discriminatory prices.[1]

The Sherman Act became law in 1890, at a time when natural price was still thought to be the general rule of the competitive economy, but when certain interferences with the natural order were beginning to be recognized.

[1] F.T.C. Docket No. 5794, July 31, 1951.

The object of the law was to prevent these restraints of trade.

Up to 1890, the competitive theory of individual bargains was not too greatly in conflict with the facts. Certainly it explained the movements of agricultural prices. It also explained the price movements of many manufactured products, which were sold for the best price obtainable. Salesmen were given wide latitude in dealing with customers—special terms, special rebates, individual prices for quantity and other considerations. As far as one can probe back into the practices of those times, the market was ruled by a catch-as-catch-can attitude, differing only from the classical price theory in that varying degrees of power were exercised by individuals. The industrial buyers were noted for their shrewdness. Even the retail stores permitted bargaining over price, the limits of which were indicated to the salesman by secret letters and symbols.

After 1890, changed conditions began to dominate at an increasing pace. By 1930, output per man-hour had tripled over that of 1890. Investment per worker had approximately doubled, according to various estimates. The mass production line poured forth a steady stream of articles. Whereas it had been simple and inexpensive to close a factory when orders slackened, this expedient now became economically and socially disastrous. As the flow of products had also to be changed from an intermittent to a continuous one, the pattern of distribution had to be rearranged to syphon off the flow at an equivalent rate. This meant the creation of a marketing system, carefully coordinated to meet the needs of classes of customers rather than individual customers. Services, rates, prices, packaging, sizes, qualities—all had to be arranged in advance in order to conform to the requirements of mass demand. Individual clever salesmanship was replaced by an administered marketing system.

The obvious widening of the gap between price theory and marketing practice has naturally led to a restudying of the controversial issues. Of these, the sharpest issue centers around the meaning of the words "competition" and, conversely, "monopoly." These investigations have been pursued in many directions, creating different schools of thought. Each of these schools casts new light on the complexity of the economy and offers an explanation of one sector. These schools are well known and need only to be enumerated as a reminder of the wide range of investigations.

1. Pure competition. A perfect competition in the classic definition; held up as an ideal by the Department of Justice and the Federal Trade Commission.

2. Monopolistic competition. Concerned with the practice of oligopolies; connected with the name of Professor Edward H. Chamberlin and developed by a large school of followers.

3. Working competition. Suggested by Professor J. M. Clark and Professor C. E. Griffin.

4. Imperfect competition. Connected with the name of Joan Robinson; has a considerable following in England.

5. Administered competition.

Discussion will be concentrated on the peculiarities of administered competition, which is limited to that group of public corporations that makes up the core of economic activities. In rapid succession, industries have converted their operations from a series of individual orders to a continuous process. Changes in design or form of products are reduced so far as possible.

In recent decades, with the coming of the continuous mass production line in manufacturing, resulting changes have taken place which have reflected themselves on the methods of distribution. No longer can manufacturers afford to rely upon the haphazard selling of their individual products as they come off the line. Systems of distribution become necessary, with organized dealers in every unit of product demand backed by stocks of goods, maintenance and repair service, spare parts, regular delivery, packages suited to the needs of customers. Only through such mass organized marketing can mass production be sustained.

Price enters into such a system only as one among various factors bearing on results. It is no longer the "natural price" which emerges from an auction as a sort of residual. It is a price fixed by management in advance, adjusted to the demand by such skills and research as are available. Since conditions surrounding the sale of the same article vary from place to place, from one class of consumers to another, and from wholesalers of various types to retailers, the price and other considerations must be adapted to fit the needs of each class. These adaptations are in terms of classes, not of individual items of sale. This is the basic distinction between auction sales and mass marketing.

Management must build its system on a long-term basis. It must be quasi-permanent as well as flexible. The effort is to build up an increasing and steady flow of sales. The effectiveness of this effort as a whole is vital to success. Every device imaginable is used to accomplish this end.

It has been found that spark plugs used as replacements are likely to be of the same type as those orginally used on the motor. Hence special inducements are offered to manufacturers to equip the motor with the particular kind in question, leading to a much lower price to the manufacturer than that named for replacement. A similar advantage of inducing replacement purchases is claimed for tires.

Certain stores are known to be leaders of fashion or novelty. They are watched and imitated. Hence an advertisement by R. H. Macy of a household item or by Saks Fifth Avenue of a new fashion item greatly eases the problem of national distribution. Such stores are constantly offered special inducements to inaugurate new items or to stimulate old ones. A contract from Sears Roebuck, A & P, or Woolworth to buy a fixed quantity over a period of time spares the manufacturer much anxiety, as well as the expense of developing new outlets. It also has its risks, for it may put the manufacturer in the uncomfortable position of having developed no alternative market. Such special arrangements have recently been uniformly condemned by the Federal Trade Commission on the ground that they lessened competition and therefore were monopolistic in character. (Morton Salt, A & P, Atlas Tires, Sears Roebuck, and Goodyear are a few examples of such special arrangements.)

How far, then, are such arrangements noncompetitive? Judged by the standard of auction competition, they are not competitive.

That mass distribution is highly competitive is the conviction of every businessman who is engaged in it. It follows a different pattern from market competition. To regard as monopolistic every form of distribution that does not conform with auction competition leads to the oddities that have been typical of the judgment of both the FTC and the Department of Justice in recent years. The extent of the monopoly built up by Atlas Supply Company is shown in the following excerpt:

Paragraph Eleven: Prior to 1930 the percentage of total sales of "TBA" (Tires batteries accessories) products sold in the United States for replacement by the Oil Companies was negligible. In the period from 1930 to 1949 the combined percentage of total sales of Standard Oil Companies has grown to approximately 10% of the total replacement sales of "TBA" products in the United States.[2]

Many people would be puzzled as to how sales of 10 percent of a product can be monopolistic. By reference to the competitive postulate this puzzle would seem to be resolved into the fact that no competitor should have any advantage over any other. This is modified only by the difference in cost permitted by the Robinson-Patman Act, which allows variations in price to the extent that there is a difference in cost of supplying different customers. How, then, can prices ever change if they must be the same for all traders? The only explanation is that they are in a constant state of flux, as demand becomes more or less insistent and as supplies come to the market in greater or lesser quantity. From this it follows that any system which impedes the flux of prices lessens competition and promotes monopoly. Not the fact, but the system is pernicious.

In contrast with the 10 percent quoted above, in the

[2] F.T.C. Docket No. 5794, July 31, 1951.

ALCOA case Judge Learned Hand stated that 90 percent control of any product was certainly monopolistic.

Are so-called "special favors" evidence of monopolistic power or of competitive power? Again quoting from the Atlas Supply company decision:

Paragraph Twelve: The effects of the adoption and use by respondents of the practices and activities hereinbefore found in Paragraphs Eight through Eleven hereof are as follows:

1. Injured, lessened and prevented competition between respondents and other oil companies and distributors, wholesalers, and jobbers, of "TBA" products in the purchase and resale thereof.

2. Eliminated competition between the Oil Companies in the purchase of "TBA" products through the Supply Company.

3. Foreclosed a large market to those manufacturers and vendors of the aforesaid products who refused to grant illegally discriminatory prices or to pay illegal commissions, brokerage, or other compensation to respondents.

4. Increased substantially the size, power, and market control of respondents in purchase and resale of "TBA" products.[3]

These standards are not sporadic. They are typical. Moreover, they condemn as monopolistic the very methods characteristic of mass distribution competition. What then are these characteristics?

1. The creation of a system.

2. Long-term contracts.

3. Effort to cultivate repeat demand.

4. Advance naming of prices by classes of customers or users.

5. Identification of special quality through trade-mark or trade name.

[3] *Ibid.*

6. Advance naming of other conditions: size of package, terms, service, replacement, regularity of delivery.

Mass distribution management concerns itself only to a minor extent with direct competitors. Its competitors are everywhere. Its main concern is to distribute as fast as the production line produces. Indirectly, managements must study whether the products of others satisfy wants better than their own—and, if so, what can be done about it. But these products need not be identical.

Throughout the economy there is found every grade of similarity in competitive articles. Cement, sugar, and aspirin are examples of complete likeness though superiority is claimed. Toilet waters, perfumes, and women's clothes are examples of likeness with actual or imputed differentials.

By its very nature, mass production and mass distribution cannot devise any formula that will produce profit maximization such as is often put into practice in auction buying and selling. Policies are adopted which operate over a wide field and over a considerable space of time. They cannot be lightly or quickly changed—there are risks in modifying adopted and widely recognized policies. These long-range conditions cannot be estimated with the accuracy needed for maximizing profits. Indeed, short-run profits made possible by some favorable chance are often harmful when they dislocate the long-term structure on which continuity is based.

There is of course direct competition among the producers of identical (or practically identical) articles and of similar lines of goods. Such competition does not manifest itself solely in price and quality, but in marketing facilities, design, and reputation as well. While in a few cases producers continue to manufacture only one line of goods year after year, recently many enterprises have spread into partial coverage of other industries. So great is this overlap that it is almost impossible to classify industries. Oil companies produce chemicals and rubber, plastics invade every field, rubber companies invade the retail field. This results in widely varying costs for the same product, dependent on the accounting methods of different companies and their allocation of overhead and depreciation. The most severe competition comes not from identical but from alternate methods or products. Coal vs. natural gas vs. fuel oil; movies vs. radio vs. television vs. magazines; leather vs. textiles vs. plastics; natural cement vs. Portland cement; chain vs. individual stores; sweets vs. cigarettes; downtown vs. suburban vs. neighborhood stores; aluminum vs. copper vs. light steel vs. plastics vs. magnesium; airmail vs. telegraph vs. long-distance telephone —the list could be expanded indefinitely. Such competition is indirect, and it results in each participant exploiting that part of the field in which he has a naturally advantageous position. The success of one does not necessarily mean the failure of another. Mass competition is not a race in that sense. It is more like a depth bomb that explodes long after it has been dropped. At times, however, one product or method disappears completely. The horse and buggy, Pintsch gas lights, naphtha launches, Sapolio, kerosene lamps, and vaudeville have disappeared (though vaudeville is being partially revived in television). More often, however, such competition results in a change of position rather than a disappearance. Technical changes endanger the position of entire industries. The introduction of natural gas has created problems for coal; television forces a new alignment of radio, newspapers, and magazines; plastics have far-reaching effects on the light metals and the natural textiles. Even the soundest industries teeter on a narrow platform. The recent decline in importance of linen and silk, of the telegraph, of coal, is noteworthy because of its startling significance.

Mass competition may be likened to the tides of the ocean, which sweep unseen in irresistible currents, whereas auction competition can be likened to ocean waves beating against a beach. Management tries to harness and direct the tides. Thus motor car manufacturers are interested in improved roads, airplane companies in accessible airfields; stores are watchful of bus and subway routes, electric light companies sell cooking and household appliances. This indirect method, often noticeable only after a period of time, perhaps obscures the reality of mass competition, and has led to the deploring of the decline of the traditional form of market competition. Indirectly, mass market competition may be just as keen as auction competition. The efforts to mitigate its destructiveness by division of markets, trade customs, ethics, threats (potential or otherwise) testify to its possible destructive character. The Robinson-Patman Act was an effort in the same direction which implicitly (but not explicitly) recognized the difference between mass market and auction competition. The protection of prices is intended specifically to encourage the building up of a system which will distribute products on a regular basis day after day. The auction competition, whereby a distributor may fix any price on articles that he sees fit, creates strains on the mass production manufacturer that are so heavy as to be unbearable. Perhaps most serious is the refusal of other retailers to display their products unless they can be assured of a reasonable degree of continuity in terms of rates of sale, delivery, and prices paid and received. This has been described as a "decline" in competition, but is it not rather a shift in the point of impact of the competition?

The test comes in the analysis of competition among "oligopolists." The Federal Trade Commission's view, logically derived from auction competition, is that oligopolists tend to act like monopolists. Certainly, in creating a system of continuous distribution, they have departed a long way from auction competition.

This is equally true whether the field is divided among three or four or among thirty or forty. Every manufacturer with a flow of production dependent on heavy capital investment must create a system of distribution which will dispose of his production at a rate in keeping therewith.

The Pittsburgh Plate Glass Company distributes through so-called "warehouses." Each warehouse must be big enough to buy in carload lots, must maintain a large stock of glass in many sizes, thicknesses, and qualities. It must be able to deliver safely, give adequate service in beveling, fabricating, and processing. Whenever there is a territory in which no independent warehouse exists or can be induced to organize, the company puts up its own. Such company warehouses account for about twenty percent of its distribution. The warehouses sell in smaller lots to dealers as well as to mirror, safety glass, and specialty manufacturers. The organization is adapted particularly to performing its function of wide coverage. The high degree of mutuality of interest between manufacturer and distributor is basic to the arrangement.

Tire distribution is more complex. Tires move to their final use through a variety of channels, each supplying maximum convenience or service to a limited proportion of consumers. This proportion is relatively steady except when a new channel is introduced, after which it settles down to another period of steadiness. In 1926 independent dealers and distributors held about 90 percent of the market. Successively, chain stores, manufacturers' stores, and oil companies entered the field and between them captured about half of the market. The new channels grew rapidly until a new stable equilibrium was established.

Each of these may offer to a greater degree than the others any one of the following: lower prices, convenience, service, choice of quality. The heterogeneous nature of the demand is met by a differentiated network of supplies. As in plate glass distribution, the system is based on the mutuality of interest of manufacturers and distributors in satisfying the variety of needs of customers.

If the system functions too slowly, the product backs up and the manufacturer becomes overloaded with stock. He must either slow down his production, or put pressure on his distributors. If, on the other hand, his distributors' orders exceed his production, he finds himself promising delivery far in advance, disappointing his customers, and opening up opportunity for a new competitor. In order to fill the gap himself he must acquire new facilities; these require time to develop. In addition, he is forced to run the risk that the demand is temporary.

In a dynamic economy, new forces are ever at hand.

They do not operate in a day, but they do operate in a year or two. New businesses are constantly gnawing at the structures of the established enterprises. The established enterprises are constantly encroaching on each other, sometimes directly, but more often indirectly with a different product that fills the same need.

The established enterprises (including the oligopolies) are more vulnerable than they appear. The great concerns do not, as Alfred Marshall said, mature and decay as do trees. They are constantly diminishing or expanding into new fields. And in this process of expanding they encroach on fields already occupied by others, causing others in turn to reshape their strategy.

Every new product must suffer losses. The overhead is greater than the initial volume can stand, yet the price cannot be geared to initial volume. It must anticipate the prospective volume. Loss must continue until a sufficient volume has been built up to cover the overhead. This may occur within a short time, or over a period of several years. In a concern having several products and introducing a new one, the established products must therefore carry the loss until such time as the new product can maintain itself and contribute its share to the total. That is common practice induced by necessity. Yet under the market competition theory it would be considered unfair—perhaps a loss leader. Needless to say, a concern having a variety of products can more easily increase this variety and carry the loss than can a new concern, formed for the purpose of innovating that same product. There are new products which are sufficiently well financed to carry the loss until plans mature. Others can take advantage of established marketing and manufacturing facilities. If it were required to price a new product initially at a profit, it would be necessary to name a price at which the product would be unsalable.

This succession of new products upsets the established order while, at the same time, those products in the process of upbuilding are solidifying their position. Not always, however, are they at the same point. Hence situations arise which give an especial advantage to a product —over quite a period of time—and which are ill described as monopolies. Once the word "monopoly" departs from its original meaning of "one," it is made to cover a variety of concepts, most of them meaningless when put to a test. They are strategic trade positions of varied strength and of varied duration. Their competitive struggle is not in terms of price but in terms of maintaining their position in relation to customer demand against all comers, ranging from similar articles to quite different articles which serve the same or a similar need. Quality, design, packaging, system of distribution—all enter into the picture. Auction competition has lessened or disappeared, but trade position competition has emerged.

In a static economy—or industry—such a situation may readily harden into long, continuous, and tight control that might well be termed the decline of competition. In this case a strategic advantage would be comparable to the monopoly power of dictating price, service, and related qualities.

In a dynamic economy changes keep undermining the established structure. The strategic advantage of one year becomes a liability the next.

Under these circumstances, the costs of preserving a strategic advantage, even after it has been won, are likely to be heavy. In a manufacturing concern, it means a research laboratory, elaborate systems for maintaining quality, methods of fostering public relations, advertising, or encouraging employee morale. In a merchandising concern the costs are also heavy. Customers are touchy and need constant nursing. Locations change. Customers move into new and distant real estate developments. Transportation facilities become less plentiful. The downtown shopping area becomes overcrowded and less accessible. A static economy based on cost has no place for research. There is no surplus for experiment.

The result of this diversified, dynamic economy is that individual corporations are constantly shifting their relative positions in industry. The giant corporations seldom go out of business, but they shrink or grow in importance and success. When they shrink too far, enough interests are concerned to effect a reorganization; and there are enough points of vantage to permit new developments. The vigorous new management which takes control can find these points of vantage from which to develop latent demand; contracts can be strenghened; products can be greatly improved with ingenuity and perhaps a minor expenditure of money. The difference between failure and success is a turn of the wrist. Unless a company has built up an insurmountable ill will, it can be steered back on the road to success. But this takes more time and capital than is generally estimated. A rough rule might be that it takes twice as much of each as is estimated.

We come back to the query: is this competition, with some sort of a prefix? It is not market competition. Yet each product definitely must win a place in an economy where others also are trying to win a place. There are no auctions. The efforts are made over a prolonged period. Gains and losses do not show on the balance sheet every day. But they accumulate. By the time they are reflected on the balance sheet, it is too late to do anything about them. In the judging of progress or retrogression, management has an inside track. It has the facts, reported daily and weekly. No outsider can possibly have a similar intimate knowledge.

Why then does management fail to judge a situation correctly? Because it lacks perspective. Managers are human, meaning that they are stubborn and emotional. They cannot judge their own efforts properly. They need a semi-informed, but detached, advisory group. This is hard to find.

What is really to be feared in the American economy is that it may become static, with no new product innovations. Then prices indeed would be market prices; then the present status of different concerns would become frozen, as in a cartel. The advantageous positions could be maintained without undue effort, for there would be no interruption. For a time (perhaps a long time) all would go well, since expense of innovation and change would be reduced or eliminated. The situation would be comparable to the freezing of types of airplanes, in order to achieve a volume of production. Obsolescence would slowly and surely take its toll, and the economy would degenerate. This would mean a decline of competition, not a replacement of market competition by strategic competition.

11

THE ROLE OF
MARKETING

MARKETING IS A SYSTEM devised to ensure a constant flow of distribution equal to the flow of production. When it fails to keep pace with production, if efforts to speed up fail, production slows down, orders are canceled, employees are laid off. Disruption and loss are widespread. Marketing is thus a concept more inclusive than the concept of salesmanship. Until the advent of a flow of production, smart salesmanship was sufficient to distribute the goods produced. The great problem was to increase production. The production manager was more important than the sales manager. But with the new technique of the assembly line, production could be increased almost at will. A reliable system of distribution took the center of the stage.

This system is planned in advance and constantly revised in detail as circumstances warrant. Outside consultants are called in. The advertising agency spreads out and establishes a new department of research. A new profession of marketing arises, and at an increasing pace it develops throughout industry. Market research becomes commonplace. The American Marketing Association was formed in 1936; by 1955 it had a total membership of over 40,000, with active groups in many cities. Members exchange experiences and search for underlying principles. Business schools establish divisions of marketing.

Marketing postulates a heterogeneous production and demand. It is concerned with the differentiation of the product and the segmentation of demand. Thus marketing has little or no place in the distribution of standardized products such as wheat, coal, and cement. It comes to its full flower in dealing with those articles tailored to suit individual or group tastes, habits, and uses. It studies the images which consumers have of themselves. It seeks new uses and adaptation for existing articles. It searches for uncultivated fields, for neglected potentialities. It thrives in those areas sometimes (and erroneously) referred to as "imperfectly" competitive but more accurately described as dependent on a strong advantageous trade position.

In supplying a segmented demand, the marketer faces a decision of policy. He can offer a variety of choices, each adapted to fit exactly the peculiar needs of each individual; or, he can concentrate on a generalized article, provided he can make it at such a low cost that the price overrides any minor disadvantages. The former is illustrated by the variety of makes, bodies, designs, and colors of automobiles at present; the latter by the Model T Ford. There are relative advantages either way, and they are differently estimated. Such estimates may be right or wrong, proved only by results.

During the 1860s most commodities were of a staple character, with only a sprinkling of imports such as Irish linen, English china, European furniture. These were of limited importance. Markets were local. Classical theory assumed that consumers were rational, so that Jeremy Bentham's theory of the balance of pleasure and pain seemed to fit the situation. Even necessities were in short supply. Bargaining and evaluating were the normal processes of the day. Prior to the 1870s, when the new standards of integrity set by Marshall Field, A. T. Stewart, and John Wanamaker became general, laxness of conscience in exact representation was widespread.

In the 1870s and 1880s the market widened. Railroad systems cheapened transportation. Communication improved. Factories replaced household production. The system of factory-wholesaler-retailer developed. Factories produced individual articles and could increase or decrease the rate of production in accord with orders which they were able to solicit. Local markets became national markets, but they remained simple. Only a few articles in the 1880s were advertised nationally—notably Sapolio, Pears Soap, Ivory Soap, and Royal Baking Powder. Frank Presbrey lists seventy-three items with "more or less" systematic publicity.

In the 1890s national markets began to solidify. Mail-order houses and department stores took on a new importance and began to put forth the claim that they were, in fact, the agent of the consumer. Manufacturers reached out over the heads of distributors to create a demand for their own products, which the distributors were thus compelled to supply. Trade-marks multiplied. Independence of choice declined. After 1900, with the increasing range of articles supplied by manufacturers and the increased complexity of materials used, consumer knowledge of value and quality became insufficient. Rational choice was no longer a guide to purchase. Consumers became too unreliable to support a system of production that was increasing in efficiency.

This situation developed in the 1920s into a struggle between manufacturers and distributors for acceptance by the consumer—whether he preferred a specific manufacturer's brand or bought on the reputation of the retail distributor. When the consumer purchases a manufacturer's brand, the store in effect becomes the manufacturer's agent. When the consumer purchases the distributor's brand, the manufacturer becomes subservient to the retail distributor. Local retailers dealing in articles of common use become of necessity subservient to manufacturers to a point analogous with agency. Specialty stores retain independence, but on a petty scale. Small manufacturers lacking a system of distribution thus become dependent on the distributors. The struggle for dominance is between the national manufacturers and the large retailers.

Certain aspects of this evolution, sketched only very broadly, require further examination.

1. With the increased variety and complexity of the articles offered, the consumer is less able to evaluate them intelligently, and he falls back on reputation as a guide. Reputation depends largely on advertising, but it also depends, as in the case of articles of frequent purchase, on the test of use. The manufacturer dares not deviate from his standards, lest dissatisfaction deprive him of the benefit of the habits he has inculcated in the consumer. "Seconds" and "off products" are commonly disposed of under another label, to avoid identification. High standards of integrity are thus essential not only to the formation, but also to the maintenance of habits.

But the consumer is not entirely helpless in so far as selection of quality is concerned. Consumer's Union claims a membership of 750,000 and estimates that it influences 4 percent of all purchases. Books are reviewed by newspapers and magazines. Clothes, drugs, and food are bought at sufficiently frequent intervals to be subject to the test of use. Pure food laws are stringently enforced. The Federal Trade Commission and Better Business Bureaus are alert to correct inaccuracies in advertising claims.

2. The rise of the new profession of market analysis thus has led to the distinction between salesmanship and marketing. The art of selling has receded in importance before the rise of so-called scientific marketing. The art of selling is old. Daniel Defoe wrote a book in 1725 entitled *The Complete English Tradesman* which is applicable to all times, even to the present. The devices of the itinerant Yankee peddler are well known.

Marketing grew out of and beyond the business of salesmanship. An advertisement of 1890 merely stated in an inch of space that "We have received a shipment of linen from Ireland which we call to the attention of our patrons." A stop-and-start economy. The unsold linen lay on the shelves of the retailer until its turn came, in due course, to be purchased. Meantime, it retained its value in the eyes of the merchant. It was not being crowded out by the arrival of more linen. When one shipment was sold out, more linen was imported. The looms in Ireland may have stood idle until new orders arrived, or they may have had so many orders on hand that they were unable to supply the last order for a year or more. The thought of enlarging their rate of production never occurred to them. But in order to induce continuous sales to meet the necessities of mass production, far greater ingenuity and organiza-

tion had to be called into being. The professional marketers could not use the whip to drive the mule—they had
to lure him with a carrot.

Marketing may not be a science, but it turns to practical
account the findings of many sciences such as psychology,
sociology, and statistics. The marketers set out to "edu-
cate" the consumer with all the skill at their command
and through every available channel.

Marketers fitted products to the desires of different
classes of consumers. They studied the quantities that
were bought. They designed attractive packages, made
displays, advertised, wrote jingles. They lubricated the
wheels of the ordering mechanism. They wrote stories
which seemed to have no relation to the product, but which
led up to the point they sought to emphasize. They created
circumstances conducive to increased use.

In an economy where industry has solved the problem
of production, so that with increased demand production
costs can be lowered, distribution may become the con-
spicious failure, the gap, in the economy. Marketing attempts to fill this gap. The crude methods of the salesmen
of lightning rods have given way to subtle and refined
methods of indirection, association, abstraction, appeals
of many kinds including vanity and utility.

3. Marketers draw a distinction between core and
fringe demand. For every established article there is a
solid core of addicted followers. In addition there is a
floating population which changes easily under pressure
or some supposed advantage. These changes are more
fully reflected in trade statistics than ever before. The
thorny task of management is to determine whether
changes are temporary and random, or whether they re-

flect a decisive trend. Major interest of course centers on the building up of a solid core. But the fringe is not ignored; it may be converted into the core.

The extent of impulse buying induced by a display or advertisement, as compared with necessity buying, varies for different kinds of articles and sizes of income. Attempts at measurement have placed it at from $\frac{1}{10}$ to $\frac{1}{6}$ of total normal sales. In either case, it is important.

Even in the purchase of durable goods, Eva Mueller (Consumer Behavior) found a surprising proportion of impulse buying. Over one third of all purchasers had a planning period of less than a month, and one sixth had a period of only a few days. There was no discussion by nearly one half the purchasers, and four fifths of the purchasers had only a little or no discussion at all. In the case of sport shirts, over a third of the purchases were reported as having been made on the "spur of the moment."

Alderson and Sessions note that "In the peculiar terminology of the appliance business, articles of substantial cost such as toasters and waffle irons are now referred to as 'impulse items.'"

A drive by one of the popular brands of cigarettes temporarily increases sales by 20 percent. The midsummer furniture sales have not only converted a dull season of the year into an average one; they have actually made it the busiest season. Mother's Day was so successful in selling flowers that it was followed by Father's Day for new neckties.

These drives do more than advance the dates of purchase or the advantage of one manufacturer or distributor at the expense of another. They leave an aftermath of increased totals. They spur productive efforts to pay for

the increased demand. They create new demands for consumption and form habits which become part of the standard of living.

4. An important part of marketing is the creation of
new wants. The range of created demands covers every
possible dimension, including adaptation of new methods,
labor saving, greater ease of living, pure ostentation. Fear
is a major instrument of persuasion. Fear of bad health,
bad breath, rough skin, being outdone by neighbors, accident, penury in old age, sickness—all are played on
endlessly and with great variety. Different persons would
classify them differently, but taken together they form
that "education" of the consumer which induces him to
purchase the products of mass manufacturing. The consumer is the beneficiary as well as the victim of the
speeding-up process.

5. It seems probable that the increase in the skill of
marketing has outstripped the skill of the consumer in
evaluating purchases. The purchaser is not always the
consumer. The purchaser represents the unity—generally
the family. When buying for himself the purchaser thinks
not only of immediate but of future consumption, especially when buying durable articles. Articles must be on
hand in order to be used sporadically. Purchase and consumption therefore are not synonymous, a point which is
greatly stressed in marketing appeal.

Marketing thus goes further than merely supplying the
demands of the consumer. It attempts to create new wants
and thus to expand all possibilities of distribution. Direct
advertising is one of the mainsprings of stimulation for
distribution. Therefore the newspapers loom large in such
campaigns, and in newspapers the bulk of advertising

appears in the Sunday editions. The Des Moines *Register* covers the state of Iowa to a degree that is exceptional. It has a daily circulation of about 200,000, compared with a Sunday circulation of over 500,000. The New York *Times* has a national circulation, especially the Sunday edition, which is replete with advertising. Its weekday circulation outside of New York is about 250,000 compared with a Sunday circulation of 750,000.

Many intelligent researches are undertaken to fill in the uncertain measurements of consumer motivations in different communities and different income groups. The proportion of purchases motivated by necessity, habit, taste, standard of living, impulse, ostentation, both in general and specifically, are anxiously sought after. The knowledge gained pays off. As the result of such a study, a local beer manufactured and used in Philadelphia more than doubled its sales in a few years in competition with the nationally known brands. Compare the lumbering complication of the mail-order blank of 1900 with the streamlined ease of 1950. Orders can be telephoned to a local agent and delivered in a few days from Atlanta or Chicago warehouses. Credit is easier. It has been found that the risk loss of consumer credit is a fraction of one percent. It is cheaper to accept this loss than to continue the expense and irritation of investigation. Systems of distribution are designed to facilitate purchasing. Credit is dispensed painlessly. Often the price of an article is not quoted, only the monthly rate of payment. Consumer response to all of these methods is so automatic that it can often be forecast with a high degree of accuracy.

6. Most important is the device of installment selling, which has reached large proportions. By this device the

time of purchase is reduced to a minor role, for the payments are spread over a long period. Payments for durable goods thus assume a regularity for the consumer on a par with his purchase of consumable items. The stimulus for having the latest model is turned into an obsession, and the old article exchanged not only becomes the first payment for the new, but also results in introducing the low-priced second-hand article to a new level of purchasers. In these ways the apparent freedom of the consumer to buy or refrain from buying comes into a considerable degree of conformity.

7. The consumption effects of the five-day week have been subjected to scrutiny and are doubtless far-reaching. In the late 1930s a department store offered each of its employees a choice of five or six workdays per week at proportionate pay. The only condition was that once the choice was made it must be adhered to for six months. The result was an almost exact 50:50 choice. In the late 1940s there could scarcely have been such a choice. By that time the five-day week was practically universal, and industry was organized on that basis. How, then, is the extra day utilized? Partly by increased time for consumption. Partly by extra occasional earnings, such as taxi-driving, repair work, odds and ends. It has become customary for certain special needs of individuals to be serviced on Saturday only, when a man is released from his regular work and free to do extra work on his own time. Further study of these proportions would be illuminating.

The increased time for consumption gives opportunity for spending that was previously unavailable. Overnight expeditions for hunting, fishing, swimming at the beaches are possible. Distances no longer present a problem. The Saturday afternoon rush becomes the Friday evening rush. Sport clothes, slacks, and lounging attire replace more formal dress and carry over into everyday life. New necessities and desires are created.

8. Estimates of the rise in productivity cluster around 2 to 3 percent per year. This is added purchasing power. Alderson and Sessions, using 2.2 percent as the annual increased hourly percentage of productivity per worker, estimate that some 20 percent is assignable to increased population; about 60 percent goes to higher living standards and 20 percent to supplying more leisure to the workers.

Marketing has thus become the keystone of the economy. The tremendous prospects of continuous production are dependent on its success. The system of distribution created by the marketers is expensive, but it is more than compensated for by the reduced costs of mass production.

12

THE ROLE OF
INVESTMENT

THE IMPACT OF INSTITUTIONAL INVESTMENT on the economy is important. New annual construction by corporations runs in the neighborhood of $20 to $35 billion, of which a large part is not necessitous but voluntary. The variation between these amounts is a determinant in future prosperity. The advance estimate of intentions of expansion and improvement collected by the Department of Commerce and McGraw-Hill are eagerly scanned, as are announcements by individual corporations of their plans for betterment. Such investments do not fructify immediately; there is a lag of several months or perhaps years before they can yield returns. Hence they are made with an eye to the future. Once made, such investments must remain fixed, and they can be judged only in terms of a decade or longer. Government investment can only roughly be separated from upkeep and consumption, but it is probably in the same order of magnitude. Together these account for approximately 15 percent of the national income. Yet new investment, depreciation, obsolescence, and maintenance have no narrow lines of distinction in corporate accounting. The federal government includes capital expenditures in its current budgets, and these are shown separately at the end of the budget document. Government "corporations" and "authorities" keep separate accounts and are separately financed. State and local financing, if large, is likely to be by specific bond issues. Whether formally they are classified as investments or long-term projects, governments have considerable leeway in their timing. Since this is more fully discussed in the next chapter, analysis in this chapter will concentrate on the role of corporate and private investment.

This concept of investment is in sharp contrast to the classical concept which centered on the individual motivation. The classical concept explained investment as a series of separate decisions, each designed to return a definite maximum. The concept put forward here is that investment is to a large degree compulsory, being made in order to create the rounded operation which is necessary to maintain or improve trade position. The urgency for and direction of investment is guided by the analysis of what is needed, whether it be broadened inventory, improved machinery, a reserve plant, an expanded distribution system or organization. As has been shown in other connections, profits are only roughly estimable, if at all.

Few major projects can be completed in less than two years; many require five years or even more. A program of development must be laid out. Such a program looks far into the future. The new construction is intended to last for many years, a matter of from ten to fifty years. Within limits it can be hastened or slowed down, according to conditions of the moment and conditions anticipated in the proximate future. It must be finished, before it can operate. Construction work is finally completed. It comes as no surprise, therefore, that new investment is an irregular factor in the economy. But the total, unless moved by a general condition, fluctuates in a rather narrow range.

The motivation governing corporate investment can be divided into two distinct categories with little overlapping —expansion and technical improvement. As the investment, once undertaken, increases without yielding a return until it is completed, freedom to curtail it after it is once undertaken diminishes.

Many diverse considerations enter into a corporate decision to expand. In the case of markets, demand is sometimes actual, but more often potential. Existent demand may in the meantime lessen or be satisfied by another alternative. Potential demand may never develop to the point expected. Plans must be capable of adjustment to the greatest extent consistent with necessities.

The Norwich Pharmacal Company is an example of vigorous development of new markets and of new products. In the mid-thirties they concentrated on the northern markets, from the East to the Midwest. South, Southwest, and Pacific Coast territories were given over to commission agents, the least expensive and the least aggressive form of marketing. Sales increased normally but slowly in these areas, thereby raising the question as to whether a marketing organization with stocks on hand, wide advertising and personnel initiative might not produce beyond normal results. The results varied. In one case, increased sales were immediate; in most cases they were delayed from four to seven years, while overhead had to be absorbed. But they finally were forthcoming. Only in one area, after seven years of effort, the results were so meager as to compel a reversion to the commission agencies. Meanwhile, expenses had increased, resulting in losses of considerable amounts.

As to products, experience with Pepto-Bismol was an illuminating example. In the late thirties, sales materially increased without effort. Here was, therefore, an article having natural acceptance. A campaign of advertising was instituted. In the next four years sales increased more slowly than advertising, and profits decreased. Then sales rose suddenly—25 to 50 percent per year—until they had quadrupled. By this time Pepto-Bismol was widely known, so the costs of advertising were relaxed. The "core" of demand had been reached, but the "fringe" was at a standstill. Another great effort in the late forties brought another large increase resulting in a normal growth thereafter.

A reversed situation illustrates the same point. For ethical reasons creditable to management, they decided to stop advertising a product that had shown continuous growth for several years. Immediately the sales dropped until after three years they had decreased by half. Expansion of markets requires a large initial investment, and is not necessarily successful.

Investment for technical reasons is more insistent than for expansion, leaving little room for choice. New methods adopted by competitors, or available to them, compel the installation of new machines and improvements. Failure to keep up with the procession leaves the corporation in a weakened trade position. Sooner or later this exacts its toll, as in the case of the New England textile industry. Chrysler's troubles in 1954 seem to have been due not only to design but also to a marketing organization which required strengthening.

In the case of the steel industry, actual shortage of production during the war, and for some years thereafter, combined with new techniques to induce an investment of $6.5 billion during the eight-year period from 1946 to 1953. This brought about an increase of 40 percent in production capacity. United States Steel Corporation alone invested $2.2 billion during those years. The new Fairless plant on the Delaware River took two and one-half years to complete from the date of breaking ground, and cost between $400 million and $500 million before it began operation. This burden had to be carried during these years.

The oil industry was similarly impelled. Insistent demand for more and higher octane gasoline forced the installation of new machinery and plants in the United States at the cost of about $25 billion during the same eight-year period. The American Telephone and Telegraph Co. had an investment in plant and equipment at the end of 1945 valued at $5.7 billion, which had increased to $13 billion by the end of 1953. The number of telephones increased from 22 to 42 million. In the same period the railroads invested $9 billion in roads and equipment, increasing their total investment by about 50 percent. In such cases the element of free choice is at a minimum. Even postponement is risky. Failure to expand and improve and not keeping step with competitors, leads to dropping behind in the procession. Undue delay jeopardizes the trade position on which the future depends.

Such decisions are not centralized, but are made by many thousands of corporate executives and boards of directors, with many specific and general conditions in mind. No precise estimates of profits are involved. The time of completion is too remote to permit that. These are matters of broad strategy which affect the trade position of the future. Nor is it at all likely that the decisions reached can be good for the individual corporation unless they are also sound for industry and helpful to the general condition of the country. The three are inextricably bound together, intertwined by many strands. The individual trader may be able to manipulate his funds in a troubled situation so that he can profit by a general misfortune, but this is not true of an organized institution.

The dominant motive is to create an organization having an advantageous location, access to raw materials and markets, and technical facilities in such combination as will permit successful operation by the management of the future. The time element over which the advantageous position is expected to last is expressed in the annual rates of depreciation accounting, varying from 10 or 15 percent on machinery to 2 or 3 percent on buildings. These rates are set according to the judgment of executives and accountants.

An industry of rising demand can absorb many errors of timing in its new investments. Overinvestment in any period is gradually adjusted, finally justifying the plans of the originators. The spectacular success anticipated is reduced to moderate success, but it is still success. The increase in population, innovations, and the rising of general welfare combine to create an expanding market, which tends to offset the errors due to overoptimism. The chemical, cement, motor, and oil industries have operated under these favorable auspices for the last generation.

Many branches of the textile, leather, and coal industries have been less fortunate. Synthetic fibers have largely replaced natural fibers; plastics have taken over many of the uses formerly supplied by leather; electricity, crude oil, and natural gas now supply much of the energy and heat previously supplied by coal. Exceptional skill of management is required to operate an old investment successfully and to encourage new investment in such industries.

Expansion of markets may be sought in either of two directions—saturating existing markets or developing new markets. Both methods are expensive, requiring new costs in anticipation of future increased sales; but the techniques are quite different. Existing markets are saturated by multiplying facilities for purchase, introducing better service, increasing to the upper limit of discretion both the quantity and variety of stocks on hand. Such tactics apply to local markets or those covering a limited area. In many localities, Coca-Cola is so easily available at every corner as almost to preclude the opportunity for any rival taste to establish a foothold. Pepsi-Cola also follows the policy of saturating a limited area, rather than scattering its shots. A & P and Safeway Stores supply many small localities so completely that any small rival has only the fringes of demand as a potential. In small areas Sears Roebuck has a like position in hardware.

Stocks sufficient to meet peak demands are greater than necessary for normal demands. A wide selection means that many items must be included for which the demand is occasional and erratic, in itself not sufficient to justify the cost of carrying. The theory behind this is that the proven ability to satisfy abnormal demand is a potent factor in ensuring the steady normal demand. It helps to concentrate all the normal demand on the spot where the abnormal can also be satisfied. It is sometimes expressed as a full-line policy, in contrast to a specialty line. General Foods, California Packing, and Standard Brands carry full lines, whereas small food processors stick to specialties. Both have position in the business of food distribution, but that of the specialties is more precarious.

Expansion of markets is quite a different proposition. It means entering a territory where facilities of distribution are lacking or insufficient. This entails investment in an organization—personnel, warehouses, supplies, advertising, displays, demonstrations.

In a sense this is a continual process, indistinguishable from the general operation of the business. Every firm constantly adapts its marketing organization to the shifts of demand and opportunity. New ideas are blended into the old, inspired by the imagination of the management. But the intensity of development varies in different periods.

Occasionally there is a definite innovation hitherto untouched—development of a new territory, a new level of demand, a new desire created. John W. Gates made his early reputation by introducing barbed wire fences into the Texas cattle ranges. He overcame doubt and apathy by widespread demonstrations of the effectiveness of barbed wire in containing cattle.

The International Harvester Company has laid great stress on the fostering of foreign markets, whereas Deere and Company has concentrated on domestic markets. Singer Manufacturing Company has a unique position of service in many parts of the world. General Motors has separate corporations in many countries to concentrate on the development of its markets, as do also the other automobile manufacturers. British Publications is an organization to develop the sale of magazines and newspapers in the United States. Possibility of expansion of markets constitutes a constant inducement for new business investment.

Quite a separate category of corporate investment is represented by the desirability of building up a reservoir or cushion of stocks on hand to be used against accident or failure of any part of the complex system to deliver its quota at the right time and place. Such a failure can result in the total disruption of the process and consequent great loss. In some industries this reserve takes on large proportions. It is an accepted rule that a lumber mill should have forty years of available timber to ensure its raw material. It is a common policy for companies in the steel industry to supply themselves with a similar reserve of ore and coal, rather than to trust to the market place. Every hospital and hotel is equipped with a spare boiler, to be used only when the heating system fails, which normally lies fallow.

An integrated oil company is in better shape than one which must buy its supplies and raw materials. To maintain its reserves, the industry explores and drills new wells many years in advance of their use. The number of producing wells in the United States has increased from 400,000 to 500,000 over the last ten years, and the annual number of completed wells is estimated to be between 40,000 and 50,000, of which about one third are dry. This reserve or fallow capital is estimated to represent between one fifth and one quarter of the total investment in the industry.

In another sense, all capital represents unused, stored up potentiality, waiting to produce. But that is not the concept developed here. Any individual item of capital can only produce at a certain rate in time, and if it is producing at this rate it is currently active. Here the distinction is drawn between such usefulness and lying completely idle until some future date when it may be converted into activity. Such time may never arrive. But the existence of strategic idle capital is still an important element of strength.

The irregularity of corporate investment, depending as it does largely on thousands of unrelated decisions, is a cause of concern regarding the stability of the economic structure. It also depends on the general economic climate and expectations. Many studies have laid bare the nature of the problem. The National Bureau of Economic Research in 1953 held a conference in which many suggestions were put forth. The main division of opinion was whether businessmen should act purely as businessmen, or whether they had a further obligation to keep the economy on an even keel by accepting their social responsibility of maintaining employment. In this respect their role is undefined, though real.

Corporate investment in technical innovation and extension of markets that need not be translated into the income statement immediately seems to constitute a source for keeping the economy on an even keel that has been recognized only recently. Government actions must always be swayed by political considerations, while corporate actions are subject to the emotionless analysis of future demands and opportunities. The activation of many half-formed plans in every corporation awaits only the leisure and necessity of bringing them to fruition. Favorable tax provision judiciously timed would bring to light many that at some time or other lie dormant. Indeed, this incentive taxing seems to have played a considerable role in the British tax bill of 1954, which offers special inducements for new investment in industrial plant and machinery. Unlike the early thirties, when the government appeared to have the only untapped resources to meet the depression, in the early fifties this potential has shifted to corporations. Government finance is already strained, whereas corporations are able to meet the inevitable interim between investment and income. Through the harassments of the last generation, corporate leadership has arrived at increased knowledge, power, and enlightenment.

It is an unsolved question as to whether the variations of corporate investment, involving as they do the general prosperity, can be smoothed out so as to constitute a relatively even flow. No single power regulates this flow. It is, however, subject to many influences, operating on the individuals who collectively make the decisions.

13

THE ROLE OF
GOVERNMENT

THE HISTORIC TRADITION concerning the role of government, which was maintained almost intact until 1930, was of a negative character. Government should, it was argued, confine itself to creating a favorable atmosphere in which industry could operate. The motto was "the less government in industry the better."

Exceptions to this general principle were few and for specific purposes. The tariff acts, the silver purchase acts, early subsidies to transcontinental railroads, franchises, patents, limited liability to corporations, the Federal Reserve System, regulation of the currency, and antitrust legislation may be mentioned. Beyond such individual activities, each of which was supposed to be in the national interest rather than group interest, government did not play an important role. Except during war, it participated in the over-all functioning of the economy in a passive rather than an active sense.

The routine responsibilities of government are well known. They include maintenance of law and order, a system of justice, a police force, national defense; a system of communication, roads and postal service, navigation aids; safety rules, building codes and sanitary regulations; a system of public education. Proper attention to these was expected to create the atmosphere in which private enterprise could flourish. Actual operation, production, and distribution were the functions of industry and individuals; their activities would bring about a wholesome, "automatic" equilibrium or stability.

Belatedly, after 1929, government found that "natural" correctives of the economy on which it had relied were inoperative or insufficient. In addition, the Hoover administration came to the conclusion that financial and industrial leaders were not equipped as they had been in 1907 under the guidance of a small and extraordinarily able group to assume the responsibility for corrective action. The new economy which had taken form during the 1920s appeared to be beyond individual or group control. The New York Federal Reserve Bank, under the influence of Governor Strong, raised the interest rate to 6 percent. President Hoover created the Reconstruction Finance Corporation and the Federal Farm Board, undertook some limited public works, and called a conference of business leaders. These seem to have been the first attempts to inject government into the economy in the role of deliberate stimulator and stabilizer. They prepared the way for still others in the Roosevelt Administration. The problem shifted from whether or not government should intervene positively to "when, where, and how far"? One venture at control or stimulation followed another in rapid succession, each designed to meet a new emergency. Inevitably, pressure groups increased their operations in every field forwarding local interests.

The federal government now plays a triple role in industry. As a direct consumer it purchases from 10 to 15 percent of the national product, and more in time of war or emergency. As a producer, it is of significant importance in many individual industries. As a regulator of business practice and structure, both under the law and by its power as consumer, the government enters every phase of the economy. The following list indicates the formidable extent of its influence.

1. The Federal Reserve Board exercises a high degree of control over the banks, which, in turn, affect the entire economy in a broad sense. This influence is exerted mainly through determining the size of commercial bank reserves by open-market policy, or through altering the rediscount rate or the required minimum reserve ratio of commercial banks. By all such measures, loan policies of banks are made easier or tighter. The Board's open-market operations affect the price of government bonds. These activities also have a direct effect on the money supply available and are probably even more important than a change in the discount rate.

The Treasury also has independent powers. It issues bills on its own initiative, in accordance with demand. This power is more latent than real; nevertheless, it exists. In addition, the Treasury names the terms for re-funding the national debt. These terms, including both interest rates and date of maturity, determine whether the bonds are attractive to private investors or whether they must be taken up by the banks; if the latter, they enter into the money supply.

Interest was pegged at a low rate for many years prior to 1953. This was done deliberately, for reasons which seemed good and sufficient to those who pegged the rate. Others thought differently, claiming that the decline in the purchasing power of the dollar was a direct result of the rate-of-interest policy. To them this was a major evil. In any case, the rate of interest was not established by natural forces but by decisions. The rest of the economy reacted to this rate and adjusted itself to it.

In spite of the fact that both the Reserve Board and the Treasury are part of the same administration, they frequently have different objectives and work at cross purposes. This was particularly notable during a number of years immediately following World War II, when the Treasury was interested in low interest rates, and the Federal Reserve Board was attempting to control the supply of money.

The tax structure and the level of taxes have an effect on the economy whether they are intended for that purpose or for revenue only. Some taxes are levied for the purpose of paying for the costs of government, others are intended to stimulate or retard the economy. In the first group belong those taxes on income which incidentally affect the distribution of individual income and corporate income and thus influence both consumption and investment. Excise taxes lay particular burdens on certain selected industries, such as liquor, tobacco, luxuries, and entertainment. Corporate income taxes show special favors by allowing deductions, as for depletion in oil and mining, exemption of gifts to educational, religious, and welfare funds.

Tax changes which are intended to affect the prosperity of the economy as a whole include manipulation of individual income tax rates, corporate tax rates, the laying on or removing of an excess profits tax. By lowering tax rates, more disbursable income is left with the consumer, thus tending to increase his purchases of consumer goods. Similarly, an increase in tax rates tends to discourage purchases. By permitting increased depreciation charges, government lowers the amount of taxable income of corporations, thus encouraging expenditures for maintenance. All such measures affect government's revenue as well as that of the consumer.

Government intervention in the economic welfare of the country was specifically pointed up in the Employment Act of 1946. This act declared that the government was charged "to promote maximum employment, production and purchasing power." But the Act went further. It emphasized growth and the fostering of free competitive enterprise. An exact definition of full employment was not attempted. The means by which the government should bring about these conditions were not specified, but they must be consistent with "other essential considerations of national policy." The constraints under which the government must operate were spelled out in the President's report of January, 1955. "It must honor the constitutional rights of individuals; it must respect the authority of the States; and it must protect the integrity of the money in which contracts are expressed and payments made."

Many branches of government participate in the framing of economic policies; but they are loosely concentrated in and coordinated by the Council of Economic Advisers. The Council is charged under the Act with continual reporting to the President and the Congress on the economic condition of the country.

2. Through a long series of acts, notably the Wagner Act

of 1935 and the Taft-Hartley Act of 1947, the Department of Labor and the National Labor Relations Board profoundly affect the bargaining techniques of unions and management, as well as wage rates and labor conditions. Bargaining practices of both union and employee are closely supervised to prevent "unfair" practices. Minimum wage rates of 75 cents per hour, later $1 per hour, with the maximum of 40 working hours per week are enforced.

As a condition for receiving a government contract, even higher minimum wage rates may be stipulated. Such contracts, totaling from 5 to 10 percent of the national product, are important in themselves; but the higher wage rates stipulated have a far-reaching effect that goes beyond the immediate cases in which they are required. They create conditions to which other industries must conform.

Wages are fixed by pressures, though often varied according to individual productivity. Maximum and minimum rates pertain to classes of workers, companies, and industries, not to individuals. The individual's rate is affected by his seniority status—confirmed by contract. There is no "natural" rate of wages. As rates of wages rise, management is pushed into labor-saving devices which greatly increase productivity, until many factories become almost automatic. Probably high wages account for a major portion of the increasing productivity of many industries. Survival is a greater spur to efficiency than is competition. The automatic factory is already here; indeed it has a technical name—"automation."

3. The Department of Agriculture has created an elaborate setup for controlling the prices and permitting the

production of many agricultural products. Through the Commodity Credit Corporation, government makes loans on basic agricultural products on a nonrecourse basis; this, in effect, is the equivalent of a purchase made at a price fixed by an arbitrary formula of parity.

In addition to this generalized participation in price control, the Department of Agriculture enters by various means into the production and pricing of many specific products. It determines the amount and price of raw sugar imports; it supervises the price decided upon for raw and processed milk, variable in different localities.

4. The Federal Trade Commission was established in 1914, but it was deprived of much of its power to issue "cease and desist" orders by a series of court decisions during the twenties. It was even denied investigative power over corporations by the Supreme Court under the Fourth Amendment. Its influence over the economy was narrowed until 1934, when President Roosevelt, by executive order, designated it as a court of appeals in disputes regarding trade pactices arising under NRA. Subsequently, its control was greatly enhanced by the Supreme Court doctrine that its decisions were based on facts which the Commission could evaluate better than the Court.

This works out to be more in action than its seemingly negative authority would promise; in some instances it positively directs the structure of industry. In the basing-point decision, the Commission ruled that the long-established practice of quoting prices at a basing point instead of f.o.b. factory was discriminatory and illegal. In this it was upheld by the Supreme Court, which held that the Commission was better equipped to assess the results of this practice than the Court. This doctrine seems to transfer final authority to the Commission. Whether or not a particular table of quantity discounts is discriminatory is also determined by the Commission. In the Morton Salt case it was ruled that the discount on the largest quantities was available only to two companies, and thereby constituted an undue competitive advantage.

Many practices previously approved were now disallowed. The scope of the antitrust laws was being extended.

Lawyers charged with the obligation of advising industrial clients regarding the legality of their acts and policies were in a state of despair. The "tendency toward monopoly" forbidden by the Sherman Act appeared to be inherent in every agreement, every custom, every pricing formula, every professional code of ethics. Normal business practices appeared to be saved only by the fact that there were not enough investigators and prosecutors in the antitrust division of the Department of Justice to bring charges for criminal acts. All manner of entrepreneurs were threatened by the sporadic indictments. Included in this group were the American Medical Association, newspaper owners, baseball leagues, the Du Pont family from the ages of eighty years to six months, trade associations, concerns using methods of pricing which resulted in uniformity and those which resulted in diversity, retailers who owned productive processes, manufacturers who owned raw materials or financed installment purchases.

Such policies widened the area in which discretion might be exercised by the antitrust authorities. The question of whether violations of the antitrust laws will in the future depend on acts that are *per se* prohibited, or whether a rule of reason will be the guiding test, is one that affects all industry. Recent decisions adverse to the government appear to limit the influence of the Commission.

Through the Department of Justice, the government challenges and frequently determines the structure of an industry and the practices of individual companies. The instrument is the consent decree. The cost of litigation is so high and its course so disturbing to many organizations that an agreement to desist often seems preferable to a prolonged legal battle. In the four years from 1944 to 1947, 31 consent decrees were promulgated; in the years 1948–51 the number rose to 75. In the three-year period from 1952 through 1954 there were 89. These consent decrees avoid an admission of guilt, but they lay down a series of prohibited practices and subject industry to the continuous supervision of the Department of Justice, enforced by the penalty of contempt of court.

5. Through the Tennessee Valley Authority and the great power dams (Hoover, McNary, and others), government enters the electric power industry directly, and indirectly the province of agriculture. Through its ownership of synthetic rubber plants the government was engaged in the rubber industry. Through its policies in disposing of wartime aluminum plants, the government has determined the structure of that industry. Through the loan policies of the Federal Housing Administration, the government stimulates or retards the construction industry.

The federal government, in conjunction with the state governments, accelerates or postpones programs for the building of schools, sewers, hospitals, roads, and other public works. Since the immediacy of these needs is relatively low, there is wide latitude in selecting the proper time to proceed.

6. The Department of Defense places industrial contracts of a great variety at approximately $30 billion annually, and in emergencies the figure may be even larger. It has wide leeway in placing these contracts in different sections of the country, in hastening or postponing construction, in controlling the stockpiling of specific commodities. This leeway gives it a significant, though limited, influence over industrial activity.

7. The power given to the President by Congress to alter import duties either upward or downward has a positive effect on individual industries. In the case of copper, the rate is specified in relation to the price. In the case of Swiss watches, the rate is raised in order to protect the structure of the domestic industry. This is a variant of stockpiling human skills in industries relating to national defense. The import rate may also be lowered in order to stimulate specific imports. The amounts spent by trade associations for gathering statistics which might influence decisions testify to the importance which industry attaches to the use of this power.

8. The Atomic Energy Commission has a place in the economy as yet incapable of measurement. This Commission of necessity has operated secretly and behind closed walls. Its total appropriation to date approximates $10 to $11 billion. Congressional committees maintain contact through secret hearings, the proceedings of which cannot be divulged.

The Commission purchases many articles of common use, and controls completely the production of many strategic metals, useful only for its purposes. Research workers on specific projects are said to number 12,000.

9. The Securities and Exchange Commission was created by the Securities Act of 1933 and the Securities Exchange Act of 1934. These acts were followed by a series of amending acts, particularly the Public Utility Holding Company Act of 1935, the Trust Indenture Act of 1939, and the Investment Act of 1940. The primary function of the Commission was to ensure full and complete disclosure of all basic facts in new security issues of corporations. This basic policy was not to protect the investor by insulating him from the risk, but to make available to him the information with which to gage the risk.

In carrying out its duties, the Commission passes on the factual independence of accountants. Before approving an issue it may order an investigation, hold conferences on alleged deficiencies, issue stop orders, conduct hearings under oath, and bring civil or criminal suits. Thus its powers extend into a twilight zone of considerable breadth. On the whole there seems to be general agreement that the results of its activities have been beneficial.

10. Up to the 1920s, the rule of capture prevailed in the oil industry. In competition with other owners, each producer took as much as possible out of the single oil pool, a part of which he owned. This breakneck speed was wasteful physically, for it rapidly exhausted the supply of oil. It was also destructive economically, for it paid no heed to existing conditions of supply and demand, stocks on hand, or prices.

Beginning about 1926, most producing states established systems of prorating; they appointed commissions under the authority of their conservation laws to regulate the flow of oil. Thus government's role in the oil industry operates through the states, not through the federal government.

The system of regulation is disconnected and irregular. Some states make no attempt at prorating. In general, these are the less important states. In California prorating is voluntary. Texas, which contributed almost one half of the total production, bears the brunt of prorating; its output over the years has increased at a lower rate than that of the rest of the country. State laws are loosely coordinated by the Interstate Oil Compact to Conserve Oil and Gas. There is no centralized guidance; each state is provided with advisory quotas prepared by the Department of the Interior. Each commission establishes monthly its own permitted quotas according to its judgment of the nature of the demands. Some may increase quotas while others decrease them. From time to time joint meetings are held for consultation and exchange of information.

This disjointed system appears to operate with effectiveness. Over the years, customs, trade practices, traditions, and consulting committees have grown up, adapted to the changing needs of industry. The necessity for regulation and cooperation is so manifest to all that prorating is generally accepted, despite occasional dissatisfaction and charges of politics.

11. Federal and state systems of unemployment insurance, even though they cover only a limited amount for a limited period, have apparently a considerable influence in maintaining purchasing power during a temporary layoff and cessation of wages. The inevitable adjustments that characterize a dynamic economy are eased over. They tend to confine disaster to localities. Purchasing power of

consumers is partially maintained, so that the troubles of one industry are checked and are less likely to spread out over a wide section of the economy.

The direct effect of these instruments of government is not dominant. Nevertheless it is very great, so that by some these instruments are described as socialistic. Just how great they are or should be, is a major source of debate. Taken together, they mark a determined step in adjusting the government to the new economy formulated by men in accordance with the prevailing atmosphere of necessity, practicality, and wisdom. In this sense the activities of government represent a break from the "natural" philosophers of the eighteenth and early nineteenth centuries; they conform more closely to the pragmatic pluralistic philosophers of the late nineteenth and twentieth centuries. Hume, Locke, Rousseau, and Bentham were replaced by James, Whitehead, and Dewey in their influence on economists. The former sought the best of all possible worlds; the latter were content with a series of adjustments to conditions. The logical systems of philosophy are replaced by pragmatism and pluralism. Nor are these objectives fixed; they can be varied from time to time. It is impossible that these interventions should all be classified as good or bad by all people. Of necessity, the individual interventions affect economic interests differently, and their immediate effects set up currents that frequently nullify their later effects.

These activities of government have led to a school of thought which forecasts their necessary spread until they result in a complete socialization of industry. If the view taken in this inquiry is correct, the shape of business practice is not determined by any underlying blueprint but by a series of decisions made by men who face a particular situation. There is no reason why each of these decisions is necessarily wise or unwise. That can be determined only by the march of time, which may lead to an extension or to a diminution of the decision taken. In this view of spontaneous growth, there seems no reason to expect an inevitable increase or decrease in the total sum of government intervention. Nor is one intervention dependent on another intervention. Each stands on its own feet in regard to its effect on the economy as a whole and the particular interest affected. It seems fair to say that the major test by which each should be judged is its effect in stabilizing the economy in the short run and its contribution to increasing production in a long-term sense. The role of government is undergoing an evolution. It has arrived at such importance in the functioning of the economy that it may not turn back to the simpler pattern, though it may still expand or contract and shift its emphasis as basic conditions and social aspirations change.

14

THE THEORY OF
BUSINESS PRACTICE

THERE REMAINS THE QUESTION of whether any fundamental
theoretical unity underlies the complexity of business practices as they exist today. As has been shown, business
practices are an individual or corporate response to a
given situation to which a solution must be found by
management in order to assure survival. The result is not
natural law but a man-made, ingenious, complicated, and
interrelated system of business practices.

This theoretical unity can be found in the universal
urge for protection against the chaotic fluctuation of the
untamed market place. The extent of protection that circumstances permit ranges from near nil to a very high
level, just short of completeness—from a limited period
of time to a long expanse of years, when the protection is
wisely fostered and not exploited. Some degree of protection, here called an advantageous trade position, is
essential to mass production and mass distribution, and it
is expressed in a continual flow of commodities. A measure
of the strength of a trade position is the maintenance or
increase of a proportionate share of the market of the
industry. A further consideration of measurement is the
growth or decline of the industry as a whole. If a decline
occurs, then the substitution of another product may be

appropriate. This leads to diversity of products within a single company.

These business practices, designed to create and maintain a trade position, have not created the best of all possible worlds. Just as they are made and operated by men, so they must be judged by men. They have departed far from the theory of a natural economy that underlay the Sherman Act of 1890.

The term "natural" economy is used in the sense of the eighteenth-century philosophers, who assumed that an automatic response brought relationships to an equilibrium which was the "natural" condition of all human relationships, including the economic. It has been perverted in antitrust discussion to apply to any situation resultant from individual actions that created by intelligence and arrangement a so-called unnatural condition of industry. These practices have largely, but not completely, freed the economy from the vagaries of the "natural" forces of the market place. An analogy might be drawn in the mastery over ocean wind that was won when the steam vessel replaced the sailing vessel. The steam vessel is still subject to storms and has its own set of dangers. It is not so completely at the mercy of the wind as was the sailing vessel. It can operate on a schedule, with a high probability of arriving on time. The navigational practices of steam vessels were for a long time derived from sailing vessels, until this incompatibility became too obviously out of accord with necessity to be continued. Since then, maritime rules and routes have been greatly changed to adjust to the new conditions.

This theory of business practice has important corollaries. In building up a trade position sufficient for survival and success, management must create and coordinate all the elements that enter into the process. This cannot be done in a day. Freedom of entry is therefore limited by the structure of the corporate unit. The designing of an article adapted to mass consumption, the erection of the equipment to manufacture it, the training of skilled workmen, and the organization and campaign to market it all take time. The coordination of these elements together with the price, the size of package, the necessary financing, and the fitting of the whole procedure into the established order is an expensive and highly skilled operation. Under such circumstances freedom of entry may be a mythical right for an individual. Entry is often facilitated through the expansion of related and already established industries such as copper and aluminum; automobiles, trucks, and harvesting machines; chemicals and oils. Structure has to do with more than mere size. For instance, corporate structure is very different in the textile, steel, telephone, and electric industries.

First in order is the process of innovation. After that comes the necessity for maintaining a balance among the varied functions. This balance is never a static balance, but one that is continually moving and shifting. Costs, prices, and volume must be coordinated with one another and fitted into a reputation and organization that will serve to carry on into the future. Profits cannot be an immediate motivation. Management cannot reckon or "take" its profits in advance. It can only create a trade position so well defined that future profits may be expected to flow from the coordination into a dynamic equilibrium of costs, prices, and volume.

These business practices cannot be assumed to be in

natural accord with social welfare. The comfortable doctrine of the classical economists that what is best for each is best for all is based on a blueprint of natural forces and does not apply to the man-made practices of spontaneous growth. The query therefore arises whether it is possible to formulate any set of legal rules or codes, based on business practices as they exist, which may serve as criteria by which to judge specific acts or structures or customs of prevailing business practice.

The structure of an industry at most occupies a secondary importance as a criterion. Competition, in the sense used in Chapter 9, appears to be the controlling factor whether there be two, seventeen, or many more units in an industry. Indeed, the closest approach to true monopoly in industry, the Aluminum Company of America (prior to the creation of the Reynolds Metal Company and the Kaiser Aluminum Company through government help) gave evidence of technical progress, low prices, and reasonable profits. At the other end of the scale, an industry with many small units and destructive bargaining market competition in the classical sense is unprogressive and unfruitful. Certain branches of the textile industry are an example. Machine shops, even barber shops, seem to have progressed only in so far as they have been supplied with better tools and equipment by other progressive industries.

Trade customs vary greatly. According to the theory of dynamic equilibrium, unrestricted trade warfare ruins everybody and retards progress. Some level of amenable practice must be found and maintained. The early trusts and cartels were a crude attempt in this direction. The series of dinners given by Judge Gary of the United States Steel Corporation for his fellow leaders in the steel industry, at which practices and codes were discussed, were on a higher plane of sophistication, though outlawed by the courts. The regulation of the output of crude oil is even more civilized.

The business practices necessary for continued survival in an era of mass production are the complete antithesis of those governing small-scale competition. Judged by the original standards of the Sherman Act they are all evil —the entire business community is guilty. At various times, judicial decisions have attempted to modify the application of the Act by the rule of reason, the degree of a restraint of trade, an interpretation of collusion, a refusal to impute conspiracy. Economists have created the concepts of monopolistic, effective, or workable competition. But the underlying theories of actual business practice are so basically opposed to the classical theory that these legal modifications touch only the fringes of the problem.

The criterion that the degree of competition increases as the number of competitors increases, and decreases as they decrease, is often applied to judge the desirability of proposed mergers. Yet this leads nowhere. Interpretation of the Sherman Act in this sense culminates in protecting the "competitor" instead of "competition"; this is quite a different matter.

The rules of "unfair competition" formulated by the Federal Trade Commission have an element of soundness, though they need some overhauling. These words are variously defined. The scope ranges from "unreasonable restriction of a competitor" to the entirety of the Sherman Act and beyond; "incipient incipiency" is a term that has been applied by the Federal Trade Commission. There can be no dispute that untruthfulness, unwarranted claims, and deceptive labels have no place among man-made business practices and should be, as they are, outlawed. Whether the method of pricing adopted by industry should be similarly controlled and, if so, how it should be controlled, is another matter. It would seem that no method of pricing is *per se* perfect. Any general policy of pricing must favor some customers and discriminate against others. F.o.b. factory, basing points, territorial prices, percentage discounts for quantity, special rates for long-term contracts, flat rates for all, prices by function—each is an advantage to some and a disadvantage to others. There can be no single perfect system. As long as each buying unit is free to make varying arrangements with others, utilizing its own trade advantage, it can perhaps protect itself in the differentiated situations that actually exist. There can be no uniformity.

On the other hand, there are limits. The ability to charge phantom freight through having a single or few basing points may lead to abuse. But this is a difficult matter. Industry in which freight constitutes a significant percentage would be limited to its own locality. Generally speaking it must go beyond the locality of its plant, even though at a freight disadvantage, in order to attain the volume necessary for economical production. Cutting prices on price-maintained articles may be disruptive, or it may be a method of passing on to the public a less costly form of distribution. A schedule of discounts may be beneficial or contrary to general welfare. A functional pricing system may be a natural reaction to conditions that prevail, or it may be a discriminatory weapon. These judgments cannot be based on an ivory-tower rule of law, but must come down to earth and examine the facts.

Indeed, not only is price uniformity impossible, it is also undesirable. Salable pricing is elementary, but it is not the only method of gaining permanence and success. As previously shown, many other considerations enter into the marketing of a product, generally outweighing price.

Management concentrates on the maintenance of an equilibrium in motion among all its elements—not on profits alone. The dominant motive in setting prices is to induce a continuous and increasing flow of demand on the part of customers. If this equilibrium can be attained— especially an expanding equilibrium—profits result as part of the flow. Profits cannot be planned in advance, for they depend on the equilibrium of all the parts that go into the unit: volume, prices, costs, experiments, research. In a permanent flow there is no way of maximizing profits, or even of knowing whether they are maximized. The only judgment that can be made is that of comparison, and through experience the result can be considered satisfactory or unsatisfactory with regard to the maintenance or improvement of trade positions.

The kind of equilibrium sought by a business enterprise that is not completely at the mercy of the market, may be compared with the equilibrium of a living organism as described by the physiologist Walter B. Cannon in his *The Wisdom of the Body*. This equilibrium he calls "homeostasis." If, for example, a man encounters a grizzly bear on a forest trail, numerous complicated changes occur in his bodily mechanism. The rate of his breathing increases, the heart rate speeds up, the blood supply flows from the internal organs to the skeletal muscles, even the composition of the blood changes so that if he is scratched or wounded it will clot more rapidly. He is, in other words, physiologically prepared either to run away at top speed or to fight. These changes accompany emotions like fear or anger. Other situations call forth other sorts of adaptive changes in the body (and mind). The living creature is in homeostasis when these changes take place only in the presence of appropriate stimuli and disappear or are replaced by other changes when other sorts of stimuli appear. When, however, inappropriate responses appear in the body, or even appropriateness persists after the situation which calls them forth changes, then homeostatic equilibrium is disturbed. In other words, the man gets sick; he may even want to die. So with a business organization.

The theory then of business practice is that from a balanced, wise interplay of all the elements involved, including innovation, a satisfactory and expanding productivity results. There are degrees of similarity or difference among companies. They are alike in only one respect —their concentration on the winning and holding of their trade position to protect them from the vagaries of the market place and safeguarding the future. This trade position cannot be maintained by restrictive agreements. Outside forces are ever disruptive. It is a dynamic concept of continuous adjustment to maintain equilibrium within shifting pressures. This is the theoretical unity underlying business practice.

From this theory of business practice several negative and several positive results emerge:

1. There are no natural automatic forces which operate with speed and inevitability to maintain the welfare of the economy.

2. There is no ideal criterion of business practice which

fits all the needs of the wide variety of particular industrial situations. The structure of an industry is irrelevant. It must vary according to necessities. The proper test of an industry is how it functions in regard to productivity, distribution, and rate of progress.

3. A trade position of an appropriate degree of strength and durability is a business requisite in order to avoid the chaotic instability of the market place. Every company plans ahead, in terms of years, for the necessary improvement of product or expansion of plant which will enable it to continue to hold its place in the industry.

4. The comfortable doctrine that the short-term interest of each individual and each group coincides with the general welfare is irreconcilable with the facts. The destructive power of each group is beyond its constructive abilities.

5. Government plays a necessary, ineluctable, and positive role in stabilizing the economy as a whole and in effecting compromises among industries and groups. There is a constant tendency for an industry or any part of it, either through changed conditions or through technical innovation, to lose equilibrium. General "boom and bust" can be avoided only by a constant restoration of the equilibrium of each industry and each set of relations.

6. The leaders of each group—industry, labor, finance, agriculture, and government—are under a double obligation to serve their group and the economy as a whole. The present practice of many leaders of each group to engage in institutionalized arguments, as exemplified by the Conference of Labor and Management in 1953, can lead only to retrogression and disaster. The purpose of such conferences is to achieve mutual understanding. Yet the pres-

sure on each individual is to state the case for his institution more baldly than he would in private conversation. This feeling that any compromise is a betrayal of one's group interest is a carry-over of the market place philosophy dominant in nineteenth-century economics. It has no place in the man-made economy of the mid-twentieth century. There is no single criterion of right or wrong. It is the responsibility of leaders not to abuse the trade position which is the lifeblood of their inherent strength. The stubborn, irreconcilable leader of 1880 and 1890 has no place in a sophisticated economy depending on compromise and wisdom.

7. There is no specified goal to reach, no blueprint to which all business practices should or can conform. Each industry must be judged in the generalized terms of its contribution to progress and social welfare. The notion that each industry and the general economy must increase at a rate of 2.9 percent per year is an *ad hoc* judgment based on questionable historic estimates.

A sympathetic government attitude is required for the operation of this equilibrium theory of business practice. During the thirties and forties this has existed in only a diminished sense. Government is as dependent on increased production as are workers, management, and consumers. Income taxes depend on income. Indeed, government does much to increase this productivity. The improvement of roads and highways, the maintenance of law and order, statistical information, the tightening or loosening of bank credit, the tariff system, the intervention in labor disputes, and protection of agriculture are all pointed in this direction.

The managers of industry do not always or necessarily

make the hoped-for wise decisions. Estimates of demand go awry, designs turn out to be unpopular. Engineering proves in practice to be faulty. Internal and external buying and selling arrangements often do not work out as expected and have to be changed. These mistakes are often of great magnitude, for the vital decisions affect a large sector of industry. Montgomery Ward adopted a policy of retrenchment after World War II, Sears Roebuck a policy of expansion. In 1954, Ford Motor sales increased, whereas Chrysler sales fell off. Handling of the national debt is a difficult matter, and errors may well lead to inflation or deflation.

The economy rests on a delicate balance of stability and innovation. For each *unit* of industry, the maintenance of this balance governs the judgment of management. Failure to keep the balance leads to deterioration and the loss of trade position.

The maintenance of a balanced, dynamic *economy* is the concern of all alike: management to retain its trade position, unions to maintain as nearly as possible maximum employment, investors to maintain a satisfactory rate of profits, government to maintain taxes.

But innovation is a double-edged sword. While it increases production, it also disrupts a certain segment temporarily. The rate of obsolescence increases, bringing loss to a certain group of investors and interruption of employment to a group of workers. A dynamic economy can never be perfect, but it can increase the total product, bringing greater comfort and shorter hours of work. Without cooperation of management, labor, and government, this cannot be brought about. Temporary losses must be considered normal, leading to a new adjustment with the expectation of a higher plane. Leaders brought up in an economy of scarcity only slowly adapt their mental attitudes to the altered concepts of a surplus economy. Herein lies the source of most present-day conflict.

This is no perfect economy. But it cannot be improved by bull-headed industrialists, government demagogy, and destructive use of the antiquated strike weapon. The growth of individual responsibility is accompanied by a growth of opportunity for personal graft—or perhaps a change in the form of graft.

Business practices may forward or retard general social welfare. Judgments may be wise or stupid in their net results as shown over a period of time. The growth of an economy based on surplus rather than shortage leads to a new set of problems unsuspected and unrelated to the nineteenth-century economic structure.

. It is appropriate at this point to measure the results of modern business practices against the classical yardsticks.

1. Does the economy operate to allocate resources to the best advantage?

2. Does the economy operate to bring satisfaction to consumers?

3. Does the economy operate to bring a reasonable stability?

In regard to the first, the economy has been put to the test of conversion to war, conversion to peace, and conversion to cold war. It has adjusted itself to each of these conditions with a high degree of speed and smoothness. For the second, putting aside any ideal of performance, it is difficult to assert that comparison with any other country or age can be interpreted other than as favorable. Individual productivity and total production, as well as a general standard of welfare, seem to be at a new peak.

In regard to stability, the record of the past has not been so reassuring. This is so because until recently the philosophy of government, businessmen, and labor leaders has been prescribed by the theories of the nineteenth century. However imperfect today's statistics may be, they are incomparably more comprehensive, more sophisticated, and more reliable than those of the 1920s. Many contributions to security, both personal, financial, and industrial have been built into the economy since 1929. Professor Arthur Cole says:

The traditional figure of a hard-bitten, selfish, asocial, if not antisocial, owner-entrepreneur, pursuing almost exclusively maximum profits, still affects our thinking. I would contend, to the contrary, that the major characteristic of business or entrepreneurial leaders over recent decades has been that of change—and change away from this figure inherited from earlier centuries. The typical businessman of 1900, let alone 1850, would feel as strange in the present business world as the typical scientist or doctor of those earlier dates, if he also could be brought back to life and placed among his professional descendants.

If the business practices have developed an economy which so amply meets the classical tests of welfare, why should they also be called on to meet the sterile tests of classic structural competition? It was during the period when classical economic and legal concepts were applied to the business practices of mass production that confusion occurred. Static concepts were applied to dynamic practices. As E. F. Howrey put it,

. . . a sensible and consistent antitrust policy depends upon the appraisal of relevant economic and marketing factors. In the absence of such information, commissions and judges are likely to continue, and perhaps to extend, the use of the *per se* approach in reaching decisions. Yet it must be obvious that competition can be judged only after the market facts have been weighed.

The conclusion follows that the welfare of the economy has been hampered by the application in law and administrative decisions of a theory of economics, the interpretation of which has no relation to the facts and necessities of business practices. Many economists recognize this. Destructive criticism of classical theory is acute and widespread. But economists have been vague and divided in constructing positive theories which might convince legislators and administrators and give them a firm base on which to make and administer a legal system. Much thought and discussion have been concentrated on a solution of this problem. It will never be solved, for new situations and innovations will constantly change specific conditions.

This is an attempt to erect a framework within which decisions will be made. The attempt is not hopeless. Indeed, it is far more hopeful to have this continuing stream of decisions made by the executives of 3,000 corporations variously selected than by a similar number of executives appointed by a single central authority.

The managers of the 3,000 great companies which influence important decisions number probably 25,000 to 30,000 individuals—to say nothing of the four million who manage small companies. They have arrived at their position of influence through a great variety of channels. Individually, they may be right or wrong, judged by the passage of time and by results. But surely they will not make great common errors, dictated from above.

Similarly, the leaders of finance, labor, agriculture, and government have arrived at their important policy-making function through many channels. They represent a diversity of experience and point of view. This diversity precludes any possibility of perfection. It is as fallible as man in general, not the concept of a single man or of a small group of men.

Is there not in such spontaneous, diversified schemata greater hope of progress than in any more molded, controlled, and blueprinted system? Errors will occur, and they will be painful, but they should not upset an entire economy. The man-made economy should continue to function through an indefinite series of progressive balances and corrections and modifications. With proper understanding there is no reason why the flow of innovations, leading to adjustment and improvements, should come to a stop. The queries of: "Where will it all end?" "Whither are we going?" "Will not this lead to socialism?" are all based on a nineteenth-century static philosophy applied to a dynamic economy. This is one danger. Another is that the rate of innovation will decrease. But the evidence indicates that the rate of innovation is accelerating, and there are indications of increased acceleration in the years to come. While the exact form of the future must remain hidden, the fact that innovation and adjustment will continue is basic in our history.

SELECTED BIBLIOGRAPHY

Abbott, Lawrence. Quality and Competition. New York: Columbia University Press, 1955.

Adams, Walter. The Structure of American Industry. New York: Macmillan, 1954.

Adelman, Morris A. "Effective Competition and the Antitrust Laws," Harvard Law Review, Vol. LXI, No. 8, September, 1948.

Alderson, Wroe, and Robert E. Sessions. Cost and Profit Outlook. Monthly house organ of Alderson & Sessions, Marketing and Management Counsel, Philadelphia, Pa.

Allen, Frederick Lewis. The Big Change. New York: Harper, 1952.

Benedict, Murray R. Farm Policies of the United States. New York: Twentieth Century Fund, 1953.

——— Can We Solve the Farm Problem? New York: Twentieth Century Fund, 1955.

Boulding, Kenneth E. A Reconstruction of Economics. New York: Wiley, 1950.

Brundage, Percival R. "Milestones on the Path of Accounting"; "Roadblocks in the Path of Accounting"; Harvard Business Review, Vol. XXIX, Nos. 4 and 5, July, September, 1951.

Cannon, Walter B. The Wisdom of the Body. New York: W. W. Norton, 1932.

Chamberlin, Edward. The Theory of Monopolistic Competition. Cambridge, Mass., Harvard University Press, 1933.

Clark, John M. Social Control of Business. New York: McGraw-Hill, 1939.

Cole, Arthur. "An Appraisal of Economic Change," *American Economic Review*, Vol. XLIV, No. 2, May, 1954.

Dean, Joel. Managerial Economics. New York: Prentice-Hall, 1951.

Defoe, Daniel. The Complete English Tradesman (1725). In *Works*, ed. by John S. Keltie. London: W. P. Nimmo, 1869.

Dennison, H. S., and J. K. Galbraith. Modern Competition and Business Policy. New York: Oxford University Press, 1938.

Dohr, James L., and Howell A. Inghram. Cost Accounting. New York: Ronald, 1946.

Drucker, Peter. The Practice of Management. New York: Harper, 1954.

Fabricant, Solomon. "Government in Economic Life," National Bureau of Economic Research, Annual Report, May, 1955.

Folk, George E. Patents and Industrial Progress. New York: Harper, 1942.

Griffin, Clare E. An Economic Approach to Antitrust Problems. New York: American Enterprise Ass'n, 1951.

Hall, F. P. Government and Business. New York: McGraw-Hill, 1939.

Hamilton, Walton H. Price and Price Policies. New York: McGraw-Hill, 1938.

Howrey, E. F. "Economic Evidence in Antitrust Cases," *Journal of Marketing*, October, 1954.

Kaplan, A. D. H. Big Enterprise in a Competitive System. Washington, D.C.: Brookings Institution, 1954.

Katonah, George. Psychological Analysis of Economic Behavior. New York: McGraw-Hill, 1951.

Lilienthal, David E. Big Business. New York: Harper, 1955.

May, George Oliver. Financial Accounting: A Distillation of Experience. New York: Macmillan, 1943.

Oppenheim, S. Chesterfield. "Federal Antitrust Legislation," *Michigan Law Review*, Vol. L, No. 8, June, 1952.

Presbrey, Frank. The History and Development of Advertising. New York: Doubleday Doran, 1929.

Robinson, Joan. The Economics of Imperfect Competition. London: Macmillan, 1946.

Stocking, George W. "The Rule of Reason, Workable Competition and Monopoly," *Yale Law Journal,* Vol. LXIV, No. 8, July, 1955.

Stocking, George W., and Myron W. Watkins. Monopoly and Free Enterprise. New York: Twentieth Century Fund, 1951.

Study Group on Business Income. Changing Concepts of Business Income. New York: Macmillan, 1952.

Toulmin, Harry A. Invention and the Law. New York: Prentice-Hall, 1936.

United States Department of Commerce. Effective Competition. A Report to the Secretary of Commerce by His Business Advisory Committee. Washington, D.C.: Government Printing Office, 1952.

United States Department of Justice. Report of the Attorney General's National Committee to Study the Antitrust Laws. Washington, D.C.: Government Printing Office, 1955.